FUNNY LITTLE GAMES

PHILIP DAVIES

J ack the Ripper achieved worldwide notoriety, not only for his nefarious activities on the streets of London, but also for the fact that he was never caught. Countless suspects have been named, plausible theories have been promulgated by self-styled experts, conjecture has metamorphosed into likelihood, but all to no avail. For over 130 years, the identity of the Whitechapel Murderer has been shrouded in mystery.

Yet all along, the unequivocal answer to this mystery has been hiding in plain sight, enticingly awaiting discovery, encoded by the killer within self-styled 'funny little games', a personal riposte to his pursuers, a secret declaration of invincibility, fuelled by a subliminal craving for self-fulfilment, frustratingly suppressed by the need for anonymity.

In 1992, an old Victorian diary was discovered in Liverpool, confessing to the Whitechapel Murders of around 110 years previously. Referred subsequently as the 'Maybrick Diary', or 'The Diary of Jack the Ripper', the author declares himself to be James Maybrick, a cotton broker from Liverpool. The authenticity of this journal has been the subject of controversy to the present day, but in the light of the ensuing revelations, the diary may now be viewed from an entirely different perspective, providing a chilling insight into the complex and ruthless mindset of a schizophrenic killer, prepared if needs be to sacrifice his own brother to escape justice.

This is the story of Michael Maybrick, born in Liverpool, family motto 'Tempus Omnia Revelat', Time Reveals All.

CHAPTERS

PART ONE

VICTIMS

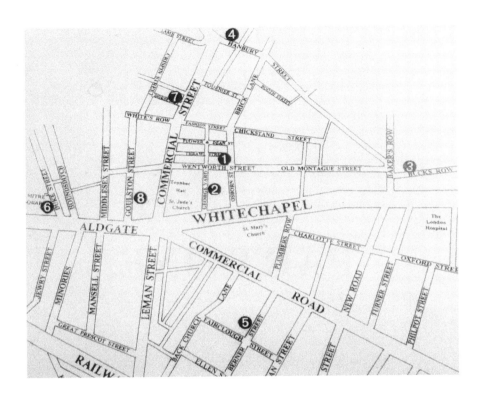

1. EMMA SMITH
2. MARTHA TABRAM
3. MARY ANN NICHOLS
4. ANNIE CHAPMAN
5. LIZ STRIDE
6. MARY ANN KELLY
(CATHERINE EDDOWES)
7. MARY JANE KELLY
8. ALICE MACKENZIE

PART ONE

WHITECHAPEL

*A London about which the ordinary Londoner is totally ignorant
...the London beyond the Aldgate pump.'* J.R. Green.

With the growth of the British Empire and a virtual dominance of global trade, Victorian London had become one of the wealthiest cities in the world, but beneath the affluence was a strata of deprivation and poverty, epitomised by London's East End, where an influx of outcasts from the industrial revolution and the arrival of immigrant ethnic groups had created a drastic increase in population, resulting in an inherent undercurrent of crime, associated with the need to simply stay alive.   Violence and robbery were commonplace, life expectancy was low, child mortality was high, and living conditions were grossly overcrowded and insanitary.   The Irish had arrived in the 1840's after the Great Potato Famine, and by the 1880's these communities were second and third generation, well established as part of the East End community, which also included descendants of French Huguenots from the late seventeenth century.   This was a melting pot of humanity, which in the 1880's attracted a further influx of Jewish refugees, fleeing from persecution in Europe and Russia, focusing on Spitalfields and Whitechapel, and bringing with them their own religion, ethical lifestyle, and inherent disposition to hard work and productivity.

The sheer volume of people in an already deprived area had the inevitable result of lowering the standard of living to pitiable levels of squalid survival.   The mortality rates for Whitechapel were twice those elsewhere in London, and 60 per cent of all deaths were of children under five years old, reflecting an environmental nightmare.   Children who survived were expected to earn their own living, selling flowers or matches, blacking shoes, running errands, begging, or stealing.

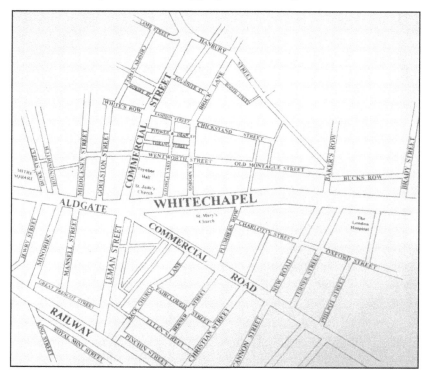

The elderly and infirm were particularly vulnerable to starvation. Many were homeless, and most lived in fear. Women had a particularly hard time, with many forced into prostitution, simply to afford a roof over their heads for the night.

Whitechapel was an area to avoid, distasteful and largely ignored, but in 1888 a series of events occurred which brought worldwide attention to the area. A devious and ruthless psychopathic serial killer was on the loose, possessed of a dual personality, and a pathological hatred of his victims. The population of London was terrified, the police proved to be powerless, and mass fear and insecurity threatened the credibility of the very Establishment. Who was this mystery man? Did he really possess anatomical knowledge, as believed by contemporary doctors and later criminologists? Were the murders spontaneous, or meticulously planned? How was he able to move around the streets of London, fearlessly and seemingly at will, without detection? Intelligence, self-confidence and physical capability would have been paramount, together with an intimate knowledge of the locality, effectively eliminating the great majority of suspects named over the years, most of whom would never have dreamed of entering Whitechapel in the dead of night.

A visitor walking up Whitechapel Road would little dream of the horrible dens within a stone's throw of the brilliantly lighted shops. It was but a few minutes after turning off the road that we found ourselves in a dark crevice like lane, with the most forbidding buildings of the slums rising on every side of us. The streets are as well paved as Broadway or New York, but some of them are no more than five feet wide. The lanes are the headquarters of the most dangerous thieves in Europe. Every class and nation is represented. At every few steps were passageways leading out of the lane, like tunnels in a mine. You could see that Dickens did not exaggerate. People unfamiliar with these districts think that Dickens drew his characters from his imagination. The man was right, Oliver Twist and Fagin were here as thick as flies. An ordinary American child would live about three days in such a place, yet there are hundreds of children that darted in and out of the passageways like rats. These are the little thieves, soon to become the big thieves of London. The atmosphere was thick and fetid, the fog hung over the alleys like lead, and the few scattering jets of gas burning along the lanes were barely visible ten steps away. Women with streaming hair and babies in their arms followed, with piteous tales and cries for money. We turned and entered one of the thousand lodging houses of the Whitechapel district. There sat the same women with somebody's babies, blaspheming and drinking spirits with the bullet-headed infants hanging over their shoulders like bundles of rags. In the presence of all the intricacies of the Whitechapel slums, the thousands of winding passageways, the tiers of bedrooms no larger than cells in a prison, the scene gave one an idea why the Whitechapel assassin has not been discovered. One might as well look along the docks of London for the rat that stole your cheese, than hunt for a criminal in this place.

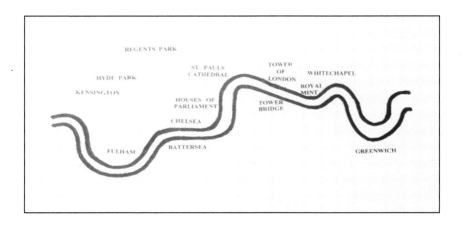

THE POSTE HOUSE

St. Peter's Church, Liverpool.

London was a prosperous city, but two hundred miles further north the thriving port of Liverpool, bolstered in the eighteenth and early nineteenth century by the slave trade, came a close second, yet it would not be until 1904 that the city witnessed the laying of the foundation stone of its first cathedral. Prior to that, Liverpool's main place of worship was St. Peter's Church, in Church Street, built in 1700. All that now remains to mark its whereabouts is a brass Maltese Cross on the pavement in busy Church Street, outside a department store. In 1856, the organist at St. Peter's Church was a musical child prodigy by the name of Michael Maybrick. Born in 1841, Michael was one of five brothers living in the family home at No.8 Church Alley, a terraced house enjoying a delightful open aspect over the church graveyard. Next door at No.9 Church Alley was the Windsor Castle public house, with rear access to the Old Post Office Place. Postal workers would come and go at will, officially or otherwise, participating in liquid breaks throughout all hours;

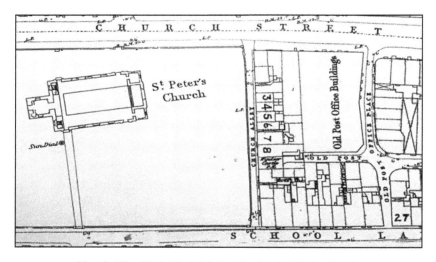

Church Alley No.8, Maybrick Family. No.9, Windsor Castle.
27 School Lane, Margaret Farrer. (Liverpool Ordnance Map 1848)

after all it was safer to drink beer than water, and much more enjoyable. A thriving little business, but not particularly conducive to a good night's sleep in the Maybrick household next door. This print by William Herdman depicts the rear of the Old Post Office Building, with the back of the Maybricks'

terraced house in the background. Just out of sight to the left of the Maybricks' house would be the rear entrance to the beerhouse, giving direct access for the postal workers.

Intriguing reference is made to the 'Poste House' in the

8

'Maybrick Diary', and its whereabouts and very existence have been widely contested, leading some to doubt the authenticity of the diary. The alehouse next door to the Maybricks' family home, however, has never been named, and should be regarded as the prime contender for the title. Over the years the Windsor Castle public house came to be listed in the Liverpool Street Directory as Rachel Falder, Licenced Victualler, 9, Church Alley.

National Census 1851. Nos. 8 and 9 Church Alley, Liverpool.

Liverpudlians have always had a penchant for pub nicknames, and there are still examples of such colloquialisms in Merseyside, the most well-known of which being 'The Vines' in Lime Street, Liverpool, known locally as 'The Big House'. In Birkenhead on the opposite side of the River Mersey, only two miles away, a notoriously rough drinking den, the 'New Dock', is known only as the 'Blood Tub', whilst the 'Vittoria Vaults' is 'The Piggy', named after an old pig farm on the site of which the pub had been built many years previously. Needless to say, none of these names are recorded in the Street Directory, and in a hundred years time those names will have disappeared into obscurity. For a beerhouse used as an informal dropping-off point for the locals' mail, the generic 'Poste House', frequented by the postal workers, was a scouse certainty, whilst in earlier years the alien 'Windsor Castle', evidently named after a ship, had always been a non-starter. The name 'Poste House' may well have been displayed over the entrance to the beerhouse, but unfortunately, whilst inns and taverns were named in the Liverpool Directories, victuallers and beerhouses remain nameless in the records.

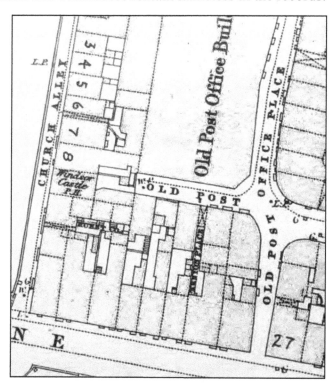

The beerhouse ceased trading in 1860, when the premises, together with the Maybrick home next door, were converted into warehouse use. However, one enterprising local, Margaret Farrer, listed in the 1859 Street Directory simply as the resident of No.27 School Lane, saw a lucrative opportunity to continue serving the post office regulars, and in the 1860 Directory became listed as Margaret Farrer, Victualler, Post Office Tavern, 27 School Lane, feted by the locals as saviour of their 'Poste House'. At the same time as the old 'Poste House' closed, the Post Office Tavern opened for trade, and in the 1870's and 80's, all the old locals, and undoubtedly Michael Maybrick, former next door neighbour of the original beerhouse, returning after a long absence, would still have referred to it as the 'Poste House', while the name lingered on. A generation later, the name association would have disappeared from usage, although the early provenance from No. 9 Church Alley is irrefutable.

THE MUSEUM OF ANATOMY

In Church Alley in the 1850's, the pub next door would have been little more than a nuisance to the Maybricks. The devoutly religious family had been dedicated musicians for at least three generations, with the boys' grandfather and father serving as parish clerks to St. Peter's Church. Young Michael was a highly intelligent and gifted musician, readily adept at composing sacred music and performing organ recitals, and, at the age of fifteen, the child genius was honoured by the appointment as organist to St. Peter's Church, a prestigious but solitary position for one so young.

The boys first attended Manesty's Lane School, which was diametrically opposite the church in School Lane, and the short walk straight after school to the solace of the church organ would have been a daily routine for Michael. Even more time was spent there at weekends, when, at meal times, mother Susannah would send one of the other boys across the church yard to call him home. Michael's capacity for composition and creativity singled him out from other children. Michael was different, enjoying the solitude of the church, where on Sundays the congregation would openly express their adulation, bolstering his self-belief in an otherwise lonely world, which, strangely enough, suited him. All his time was spent close to home and church, and even his sheet music came from just over the road at No. 63 Church Street, where Stephen Adams ran the local booksellers and stationery business.   Stephen was ten years older than Michael, and evidently quite a rapport was built up between the two.   Neither would have known at the time that the name of Stephen Adams would eventually achieve national renown and international acclaim. Not for Michael the confines of a small room at home, with ill-fitting sash window overlooking a noisy post office yard, but lofty stained glass windows, and hours of solitary single-minded dedication.   The church organ was his private sanctuary, his seat of meditation, where he would privately share deep thoughts with guiding spirits, his divine inspiration.   Michael was very special, and knew it.

In 1860 there arrived in Liverpool a flamboyant American showman by the name of 'Dr.' Joseph Woodhead, master of chicanery and purveyor of snake oil remedies for all ills, bringing with him 'The Museum of Anatomy', which he located at 29 Paradise Street, less than one minute's walk away from St. Peter's Church.

Amongst items of morbid interest displayed in the museum were realistic wax models of naked young women, with innards exposed to reveal the structure of the internal organs, which at set times would be taken apart and re-assembled by an assistant, accompanied by a medical dialogue. Ladies were admitted for a three hour period on Tuesdays and Fridays, and, needless to say, objections were raised by some as to the pornographic nature of the displays.

Joseph Woodhead had clearly anticipated this hurdle, and complemented the 'medical' displays with puritanical religious references relating to the purification of the soul, allowing patrons to adhere to the narrow path of righteousness, whilst savouring the prurient delights on offer. *'If any man defile the Temple of God, him will God destroy.'*

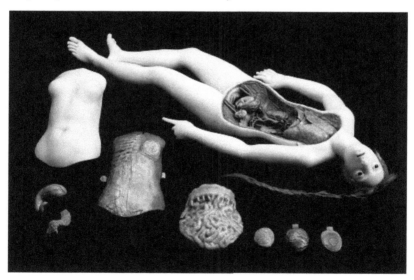

Wax model with moveable viscera.

Graphic displays were for the enlightenment of the soul, rather than titillation. In an age when the display of a bare ankle was regarded as risqué, the wax ladies of the museum proved a great success, and the spiritually enlightened male population of Liverpool, young and old, ensured a regular income for Joseph Woodhead. Further along the corridor from the anatomical displays were graphic sections relating to venereal disease and masturbation, referred to as 'onanism'. The graphic dialogue reads as follows:

Would there be no necessity of speaking on this delicate subject, but must we, for the sake of mere delicacy, or even from higher consideration of interest or self-applause, conceal from ourselves and others, the latent cause of misery and death to tens of thousands? The frightful consequences of self- pollution who can depict? Continued weariness, weakness, aversion to exercise and business, dimness and dizziness of sight, paleness, impotency, barrenness, palpitation of the heart, trembling, loss of memory, are they not fearful, and do they not proceed from this cause?

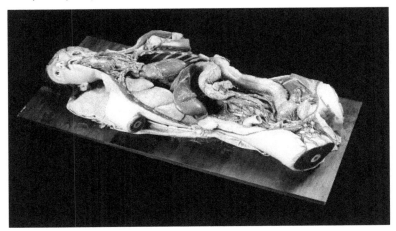

Wax model with moveable viscera.

Commencing in youth, continued at school, and persevered in maturity, this dreadful pernicious habit makes its inroads on the constitution just when the powers of life would otherwise have been fully and happily developed. How sedulously should parents – the guardians of youth – our teachers – and all concerned in the future welfare of society, keep their guard over this evil. In many respects it is several degrees worse than common whoredom. It excites the power of nature to undue action; hence the muscles become flaccid and feeble, the tone and natural action of the  *nerves are relaxed and impeded, the judgment perverted, the will indeterminate and wholly without energy; the eyes appear languishing and without expression, and the countenance vacant; appetite ceases, for the stomach is incapable of performing its proper office. Nutrition fails, tremors, fears and terrors are generated, and thus the wretched victim drags out existence, till even before his time to arrive at man's estate, with a mind often debilitated, even to a state of idiotism, his worthless body tumbles into the grave, and his guilty soul is hurled into the awful presence of God.*

Could the above explain the high male mortality rate in Liverpool? A visit to the museum must have put the fear of God into the minds of young men living within the pious moral constraints of Victorian England. Many a sleepless night would have been spent by the more impressionable of the museum's younger clientele, educated in the principals of religion, yet torn by the primaeval need to procreate …. or even to kiss a girl?

'Worse than common whoredom'? Was this not tacit acknowledgement that common whoredom was more acceptable than the tempting alternative of 'onanism'? Did Michael visit the museum in early adulthood, purely for educational purposes, of course, befriending the assistant and even being allowed the opportunity of intimately examining the internal parts, dissembling and reassembling, familiarising himself with the anatomy of the lifeless female forms? Had he taken seriously Woodhead's nonsensical rhetoric on onanism? Did he venture forth late one night to taste the forbidden fruit of a Maggie May, strolling under the gas lights of Lime Street in the city centre, or loitering around the dark dockland honeypots of Brick Street and Jamaica Street. He would certainly not have been the first young man to give it a try, followed a few days later by another visit the Museum of Anatomy, only this time to study the terrifying consequences of venereal disease.

> 261. – Face of an old bachelor: a confirmed onanist. He became idiotic, and rapidly sank into second childhood. (What a fearful account he will have to give of himself at the judgement day).
>
> 262. – Face of a man shewing the evil effects of secondary symptoms of syphilis.
>
> 263. – Syphilis case. This model of the head represents the final and most severe form of secondary symptoms, with the palate lost, the bones of the nose destroyed, and the whole system a perfect mass of corruption.

Inside the hyper-active mind of the young musical genius exploded the worst trauma imaginable. Curse the whore! The family doctor would invariably have been a member of the congregation, and certainly not one whose confidentiality could be trusted on this delicate subject. Various forms of sexually transmitted disease were on offer from the seductive street-corner sirens of late night Liverpool, resulting in severe discomfort and impotency, and whilst antibiotics and psychotherapy are readily available now, in the 1850's neither was an option. Unbeknown to the victims of the day, syphilis would sometimes lie dormant within the body only to cause severe psychological trauma in later life.

Symptoms of neurosyphilis can appear decades after infection, and can cause lasting issues including general paresis, leading to health problems including paranoia, mood swings, emotional troubles and personality changes.

Teresa Burger. University of Illinois. College of Medicine.

Best pack the bags and seek discreet treatment on the continent, rather than face possible discovery at the Seaman's Mission in Liverpool. It was 1865, and time for a career move in any event. Damn the whore!   So Michael, 24 years old, and a recently qualified Professor of Music, left Liverpool to further his career in Germany.   Whilst Michael's future looked promising, that of his friend Stephen Adams went into severe decline.   In July 1863, Stephen had been declared bankrupt, and news of Michael's imminent departure was a further blow. Had Michael's late night dalliance caused friction between the two? Theirs was a very special relationship which no-one else

C. H. KEENE, Registrar.

NOTICE is hereby given, that the following is a copy of an entry made in the book kept by the Chief Registrar of the Court of Bankruptcy for the registration of Trust Deeds for the benefit of creditors, Composition and Inspectorship Deeds executed by a debtor, as required by the Bankruptcy Act, 1861, secs. 187, 192, 194, 196, and 198 :—

Number—4931.

Title of Deed, whether Deed of Assignment, Composition, or Inspectorship — Deed of Composition and Release.

Date of Deed—15th June, 1863.

Date of execution by Debtor—9th July, 1863.

Name and description, as in the Deed—Stephen Adams, of No. 63, Church-street, Liverpool, in the county of Lancaster, Bookseller and Stationer.

The names and descriptions of the Trustees or other parties to the Deed, not including the Creditors—The several persons whose names and seals are subscribed and affixed and who are respectively creditors of the said debtor.

A short statement of the nature of the Deed—Agreement by the creditors to accept a composition of six shillings in the pound, upon and in satisfaction and discharge of their respective debts, to be paid by two instalments, namely; three shillings in the pound on the execution of the deed and three shillings at the expiration of three months from the 15th June last past, to be secured by the promissory notes of the debtor, and a release from the creditors to the debtor from the debts owing by him to them and all remedies for recovery thereof, save only and except such rights and remedies as are given or secured to them under or by virtue of the same promissory notes.

When left for Registration — 10th July, 1863, at 3 o'clock.

C. H. KEENE, Registrar.

18

understood, given the strictures of Victorian England. The good old days were over, and life would never be the same. The Museum of Anatomy survived for another seventy years in Liverpool, following which the business was moved to a more lucrative site in the holiday resort of Blackpool, and thence to nearby Morecambe, as part of Madam Tussaud's, where in the 1960's one young man admitted to spending many an hour in the museum, where the displays had changed little since the 1850's.

It was a rare visit when he didn't find time to call in at Tussaud's to see if there was 'owt fresh in'. There rarely was. The Museum of Anatomy is a grandiose title for the two rather small, dimly lit and musty chambers that the title embraces. Negotiating the sort of frosted glass 'modesty' screen often erected at the entrance to public lavatories, the visitor finds himself standing in a room whose first assault is on the nostrils. Being Victorian and therefore much prized by the Museum's owner for their 'antique' value, the exhibits here are fashioned of ordinary candlewax. Stepping out of the 'Museum of Anatomy', the visitor is confronted with a full scale replica of Christ on the cross, whose brightness, after the half-dark, seems almost blinding. Somebody's Husband, Somebody's Son. Gordon Burn.

The young man was Peter Sutcliffe, who in the 1970's contracted a venereal disease from a local prostitute, and, as the Yorkshire Ripper, wreaked personal vengeance by murdering at least thirteen more, inspired by a controlling 'voice' which told him to rid the streets of prostitutes. His father wrote of him, *'Peter was just a quiet little lad, that's all. He didn't have any sort of affectations. None at all. No affectations whatsoever.'*

ORPHEUS AND EURYDICE

MICHAEL MAYBRICK

Michael Maybrick duly embarked on a musical venture across Europe, travelling alone to Leipzig, where he studied musical composition under Hans Richter, followed by a period at the Milan Conservatory under Giatano Nava, during which time the virtuoso discovered Michael's potential as a baritone singer, which soon became his new vocation. After appearances at minor theatres in Northern Italy, he returned to England, touring with the acclaimed Carl Rosa Opera Company, and performing alongside the eminent baritone Charles Santley, also from Liverpool. The pair bonded immediately, and Charles introduced Michael to the renowned impresario, music publisher, and lover of fine wines, John Boosey, who would later prove instrumental to his career. Michael next appeared in London to great acclaim as the leading role in Mendelsohn's 'Elijah', at the culmination of which, with black beard and flowing robes, he was whisked away to the theatrical heavens in a fiery chariot.

The production ranked second only to Handel's 'Messiah' in public acclaim at the time, and Michael Maybrick's performance was greeted enthusiastically. Energy and adulation drawn from rapturous audiences, culminating in Elijah's transformation into a spiritual entity, had a profound effect on this deeply intense young man, steeped in a religious background, alone with his thoughts and 'voices'.

Did Michael Maybrick come to believe he had a spiritual link with Elijah? There are well documented examples of such effects on behavioural patterns, one of the most striking examples in recent years being that of the actor Jeremy Brett, who played Sherlock Holmes in the Granada Television series, produced between 1984 and 1994. During the course of the series, the actor became increasingly drawn to the title role, slowly developing a dual personality disorder, and ultimately succumbing to severe psychological problems as a consequence.

Some actors fear if they play Sherlock Holmes for a long run, the original character will steal their soul, leaving no corner for the original inhabitant ... Holmes has become the dark side of the moon for me. He is moody, solitary, and underneath I am really social and gregarious. Jeremy Brett.

In similar vein, Michael Maybrick may well have nurtured self-belief as a disciple of Elijah, the source of 'voices' which he believed controlled his destiny. Three religious figures in the scriptures experienced the fiery whirlwind and accompanying flight to the heavens, or the 'New Jerusalem', namely Elijah, Ezekiel and St. John the Divine, living centuries apart. Coming as he did from a devoutly religious family, all would have been familiar to Michael Maybrick from an early age, and would soon play a major part in the increasingly dark side of his psyche.

And it came to pass, as they still went on and talked, that behold there appeared a chariot of fire, and horses of fire, and parted them both asunder, and Elijah went up by a whirlwind into heaven.   Kings 2.11.

And I saw a likeness as the beholding of fire .... and the likeness of a hand was sent out and took me by the hair of my head, and the spirit raised me up betwixt heaven and earth, and brought me into Jerusalem.   Ezekiel 8.13.

After these things I saw, and a door was opened in heaven, and the first voice that I heard was as a trumpet speaking with me .... and at once I was in spirit, and a seat was set in heaven.
                                          Revelation 4. 1-2.

And I saw a new heaven and a new earth, and I, John, saw the holy city Jerusalem coming down from heaven, made ready as a wife adorned to her husband.   Revelation 21. 1-2.

As well as prophesies of doom, Ezekiel reserved drastic punishment for whores, a trait of which Michael Maybrick thoroughly approved, creating an even greater affinity with his icon. Women were no part of his world, and he could well do without them. With every passing year, his public persona metamorphosed into one of self-importance and pomposity, and were it not for sycophantic admirers of his musical talents, he would have attracted few friends. Although content in his own company, in the late 1870's he developed a close rapport with barrister Frederick Weatherly, and the duo discovered a flair for composing musical ditties, sea shanties and ballads. Initially, this was alien to the operatically trained and inherently serious baritone, but opposites attract, and the genial Fred must have sparked a fire within, resulting in a musical chemistry which would transform Michael's career yet again. Soon he was equally as adept in the music hall as in the opera house, gaining a reputation as one of London's most eligible bachelors, rendered even more attractive by his resistance to the ladies' charms.

Intriguingly, before publishing any of their works, Michael adopted a change of identity for the purpose of composing ballads, using the pseudonym of his boyhood friend Stephen Adams, bankrupted in 1863, shortly before Michael left for the continent. Did Michael feel responsible for the demise of his friend, more than a friend, the only person who really understood him, who appreciated he was different? Stephen had lost heart at Michael's departure from his life, and as business declined, had to leave behind his prestigious Church Street premises for a humble location in West Derby, on the outskirts of Liverpool. The bookseller's life had been the complete antithesis of Michael's, and by the mid 1870's Stephen's health had failed. Were the couple still in touch, was Michael helping to support him, empathising with his fall from high street profile to back-street obscurity? Did Michael Maybrick have an affectionate side to his character, strictly reserved for male friends in private? Distinctly possible, if not highly likely.

The first musical composition by Stephen Adams to achieve a modicum of success was the patriotic ballad, 'A Warrior Bold', credited to a lyricist named Edwin Thomas, of whom there is no record in the musical chronicles. The man seemingly does not exist, and it begs the question as to whether this is another pseudonym, based on the names of Michael's two younger brothers, Edwin and Thomas? All royalties to Michael, thank you. Did Michael Maybrick divert the occasional modest royalty cheque from other compositions, made payable to Stephen Adams, to arrive in the post in West Derby, Liverpool, with nobody the wiser except the pair from Church Alley and Church Street? An invisible bond, a hand of friendship, and a gesture of re-assurance over the miles, delivered by post. This would explain the otherwise unaccountable change of name, well before fame would permanently and irreversibly seal the arrangement.

In later years, the following article appeared in 'The New Penny Magazine', recounting Maybrick's lame and implausibly contrived explanation of the name change.

Michael Maybrick has always had a great success in singing his own compositions. It was to avoid any invidious remarks on the subject that he assumed a nom de plume. The selection of the one he adopted came about in the most casual manner whilst discussing his earliest publication with the house of Chappell. 'What name will you take?' 'What's in a name? Call me anything you like.' 'No, choose one for yourself – any, the first you think of will do.' 'Well then, Adam, the first of all names, is the one I select.' 'Make it Adams, and put something before it.' 'Now, who shall be called upon to stand godfather to this child of the imagination? Stephen Heller? Why not, since I love his music. So let me be Stephen Adams.
.   New Penny Magazine.

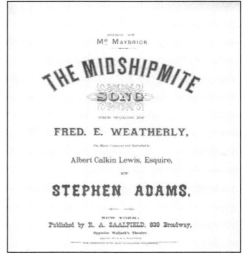

SUNG BY
MR MAYBRICK

THE MIDSHIPMITE
SONG

THE WORDS BY

FRED. E. WEATHERLY,

The Music Composed and Dedicated to

Albert Calkin Lewis, Esquire,

BY

STEPHEN ADAMS.

NEW YORK:
Published by R. A. SAALFIELD, 833 Broadway,
Opposite Wallack's Theatre.

The music sheet for the 'Midshipmite' illustrates the dual yet separate entities of the singer 'Mr. Maybrick' and the composer Stephen Adams, believed by the general public in the early days to be two separate people. Could the need for an alter ego have been an early sign of a split personality? Only when Nancy Lee was published in 1876, and the duo achieved

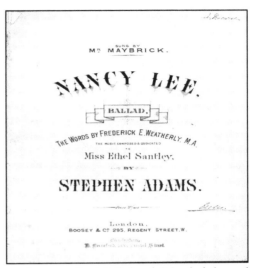

national fame, did it become known that Michael Maybrick and Stephen Adams were one and the same person. Stephen Adams was definitely here to stay.

It will not have been forgotten that Mr. Maybrick displayed early talent for composition, but it is not until 1876 that it was reserved for 'Stephen Adams' to produce a ballad that is probably the most successful ever written. No song has ever gained such enormous popularity as Nancy Lee. Everyone was singing it, humming it, or whistling it in the street, drummed into every ear, morning, noon and night. Mr. Maybrick has much to answer for in having given forth this inspiration to the world, for it seems to have fallen like a spell on every individual capable of making musical sounds. New Era,   14 September 1878.

In February 1878, the mortal remains of the late Stephen Adams were laid to rest in the obscurity of a West Derby cemetery, whilst the name lived on, rising swiftly to international fame.   By the early 1880's Stephen Adams and Fred Weatherly were as renowned as their operatic contempories, Gilbert and Sullivan, and whilst Fred shunned the limelight, Michael Maybrick basked in glory, spending many a social hour mingling with the rich and famous, including his now close friend, Sir Arthur Sullivan.

Nowhere in London was better suited for such occasions than the gentleman's club, offering 'home from home', where gentlemen would socialise and dine in fine surroundings in a totally male environment, ideally suited to the confirmed bachelor. The London clubs varied immensely in status, dependent on the calibre of membership, and a select number were particularly renowned, including the exclusive and unconventional Savage Club in Adelphi Terrace, into whose portals Michael Maybrick gained admission in 1880. The club revelled in pushing the boundaries of accepted propriety, and raucous behaviour in controlled measure was ever such fun behind closed doors.

As to the many explanations as to the name, my brother Robert suggested 'Savage Club' as we are all Bohemians and assembled in the precincts where Richard Savage, prince of

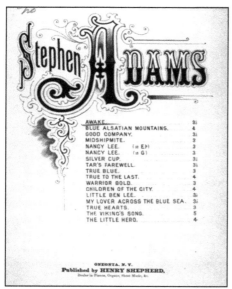

Bohemians died. Besides, said my brother, we can call ourselves savages because we are outside the pale of civilisation.
William Brough. Founder Member.

On occasions, the club would hold entertainment evenings dedicated to the serious business of smoking, drinking, and general frivolity, as depicted in the following scene in the Illustrated London News. No less a figure than HRH Edward, Prince of Wales, was a regular at the Savage, on the top left of the picture, whilst second right, middle row, on the piano, is Michael Maybrick, exploiting every opportunity to advance his position in the highest circles of London society. The boy organist from Church Alley, Liverpool, was now very well connected indeed. Amongst fellow club members at the time were Sir Frederic Leighton, the greatest living artist and sculptor of the Victorian era, Sir Arthur Sullivan, of Gilbert and Sullivan fame, and Dr. Frederick Gordon Brown, City of London Police Surgeon, who was soon to figure in the impending Whitechapel murders.

Equally prized as membership of a gentleman's club was admission into a Masonic Lodge, governed by the United

Grand Lodge of England, Great Queen Street, London. In Victorian England, membership was particularly selective, not broadly advertised outside the craft, as it was known, and operating through a system of individual Lodges subservient to their respective Provincial Grand Lodge, all of which in turn were under the leadership of the Grand Master, traditionally

HRH Edward Prince of Wales and HRH Albert Victor.

a member of the Royal family. Since 1874, the position had been occupied by HRH Edward Prince of Wales, later to be crowned King Edward VII.

In the higher echelons of Freemasonry, ensconced in carefully selected Lodges, were to be found members of the Establishment, military, church, judiciary, politics, journalism and the arts. Inter-lodge invitation formed webs of contact, united by secrecy, fraternity and obedience to the principals of the craft. As a general rule, in Victorian times, the lower the Lodge number, the older and more select was the Lodge, each of which was subject to strict rules of protocol, governed by the United Grand Lodge of England, based on an adherence to moral and spiritual enlightenment and advancement of social cohesion. Much was discussed behind closed doors, and secrecy within the brotherhood was seen as paramount, protected by solemn oaths sworn by initiates on admittance to the Order.

Michael Maybrick, to all external appearances, would have appeared an ideal candidate. The Savage Club had its own associated Masonic Lodge, Savage Lodge No.2190, membership of which included Sir Arthur Sullivan and HRH Albert Victor, Duke of Clarence, a confirmed bachelor, and a name at one time associated with the Whitechapel murders, for no valid reason whatsoever, simply suspicion of the secrecy afforded by Freemasonry. Michael Maybrick ventured into Freemasonry in 1876, when initiated into Athenaeum Lodge No.1491, meeting at the Athenaeum, Islington, London, subsequently joining St. Andrews Lodge No.231, meeting at Freemasons Hall, Great Queen Street, London. In August 1877, Michael Maybrick organised the formation of a new Masonic Lodge, musically orientated, and named after a mythological minstrel from Greek legend, renowned less for his musical skills than for his descent into the underworld, a character well suited to the increasingly deep psyche of the principal founder member. The Orpheus Lodge No.1706 was consecrated in Freemasons Hall, Great Queen Street, London, meeting there until 1886, when the decision was taken to move to less formal surroundings in the Holborn Restaurant, Holborn. Four years later, Michael Maybrick founded Eurydice Lodge No.1920, named after Orpheus's lost love, meeting at the Oak Hotel, Surbiton, Surrey, 'for those interested in the pursuit of sports.'

When Stephen Adams is not working, he is either drilling at Somerset House, imbibing ozone at his Isle of Wight Cottage, rowing on the Thames, riding over Highgate Hill, or enjoying the conviviality of the Arts Club. He regards his exercise out of doors, and the social evenings he spends at one or other of his clubs, as the most welcome preparation for his labours at home.

New York World. 15 January 1891.

A prominent feature of Freemasonry is the conviviality afforded by invitation to different Lodges, with reciprocation offering the opportunity of extending circles of friendship. Michael Maybrick, however, saw the Order as a potential source of advancement in a relentless crusade for personal recognition which knew no bounds. Fame was his destiny.

A WARRIOR BOLD

St. Jude's Church and Vicarage, Commercial Street, Whitechapel, 1873.

The distance between Whitechapel and the Bank of England is less than a mile, and nothing could more graphically represent the class divide in 19th century London. Social awareness at the time had prompted the wealthy of a more generous disposition to fund charities, alleviating the dire conditions in East London by providing free education, care for the homeless, and job creation for the destitute unemployed. In 1865, William Booth had opened a Christian Mission in Whitechapel, evolving eventually into the Salvation Army, whilst two years later, Dr. Thomas Barnardo was so affected by the sight of bare-footed children in rags, sleeping in gutters and sheds, that in 1867 he founded an institution, which, over the next forty years, would care for over 8,500 children. Other philanthropists soon extended their generosity, and more charitable foundations and relief organisations sprang up, supplementing subsistence measures provided by local parishes and churches, providing some measure of respite in an otherwise forlorn existence. One such institution was situated just north of the junction between Whitechapel and Commercial Street, where in 1873, the Rev. Samuel Barnett applied for permission to take over the neglected and disused St. Jude's Church, where he and his wife

Henrietta embarked on a lifetime's mission, to enlighten the lives of underprivileged locals in one of the most deprived areas in the country.

In 1883, the couple acquired the land immediately adjoining the church, occupied by a Boy's Refuge and Industrial School, funded by local brewers Truman, Hanbury and Co; and caring for orphans and severely deprived children, sleeping in a rectory dormitory in nearby Colchester Street. Following a fire in 1883, the school was closed, and the Barnetts seized the opportunity to expand their project of social reform by proposing the construction of Toynbee Hall, dedicated to the memory of fellow reformer Arnold Toynbee. The Rev. Samuel Barnett had studied at Cambridge University, later befriending fellow students, not

least of whom was the Duke of Clarence, Prince Albert Victor Edward, 'Prince Eddy' to his friends. During his first term at Cambridge, the Prince became involved in the Toynbee Hall project, enticing a following of well-heeled undergraduates from both Oxford and Cambridge to unite in a project to improve the conditions of the poor in London's East End. By siting the building in the heart of impoverished Whitechapel, the students would be immersed in a totally alien environment, introducing the rich and privileged to the reality of poverty, and offering the opportunity of providing some level of aspiration for youngsters trapped in an otherwise desperate existence.

They come to learn as much as to teach ... there is nothing like contact for giving or getting understanding. Henrietta Barnett.

So impressed was Prince Albert Victor that he undertook to head the Toynbee Hall Association, liaising with the Rev. Samuel Barnett in the development of the venture, a catalyst for social reform which extended beyond basic education to outward bound courses, singing classes, military drill for boys, and hopefully the path to a more positive future. The Royal connection invariably attracted artists and celebrities keen to lend support, and Toynbee Hall became quite a cause celebre within London society.

Last summer, several concerts were given in the quad, with enthusiastic audiences of three or four hundred. This year, six evenings have seen our quadrangles lit up with chains of coloured lamps and Chinese lanterns, and the band playing.

Once the kindness of Col. the Hon. Paul Methuen gave us the pipes of his regiment. The other evenings, the artists band, the police band, and Mr. Freeman Wills' band played for us. The audiences are very large, and would satisfy the most ardent advocate of all sorts and conditions, and nowhere is the pleasure more universal or genuine.

Paul Metheun was an ardent Freemason, member of Trafalgar Lodge No.971, Windsor Castle Lodge No.771, and Wanderers Lodge No.1604, and the artists band to which reference is made is that of the 20th Middlesex (Artists) Rifle Volunteers Regiment. Such volunteer regiments were the predecessors of the present day Territorial Army, formed on the recommendation of the area's Lord Lieutenant, with members providing their own arms and equipment, purchased under the superintendence of the War Office to ensure uniformity of arms. Whilst in the formative years the unit was hardly the sharp end of the country's fighting force, over the years the regiment was destined to boast many fine members, including Leander Starr Jameson, leader of Jameson's Raiders in the Boer War, of whom Rudyard Kipling, Freemason and founder member of Lodge No.12, St. Omer, France, wrote the epic poem with the stoic opening line *'If you can keep your head when all about you are losing theirs and blaming it on you.'* Sixty years later, the 20th Middlesex Volunteers would develop into the Special Air

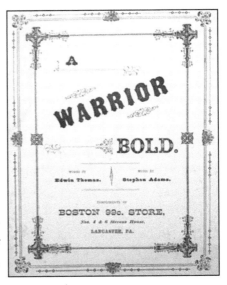

Service Regiment, attached to the SAS, the most elite fighting force in the world. The band of the Artists Rifle Volunteers performed regularly at Toynbee Hall, and Colonel Paul Methuen's patronage ensured the attendance of celebrity guests, including close friend Colonel Robert Edis of the 20th Middlesex, of whom a contemporary article records,

Colonel Edis seemed to be acquainted with a vast number of distinguished people of every rank and profession, from Royalty downwards. I can also well recollect the evenings 'at home' given by Sir Robert, at which all the notables in Art, Literature and Drama might be met. Some very fine smoking concerts were arranged at which some of the best talent in London gave their services, including Lionel Gough, Brandon Thomas, Michael Maybrick, and many others. During his period of command, many notable persons visited us, not only the Prince of Wales, but the Duke of Cambridge, Lord Roberts, Lord Wolseley, and Lord Metheun. Memories of the Artists Volunteers. Col. H.A.R. May.

Robert Edis was a notable Freemason, Past Master of Westminster and Keystone Lodge No.1118, Drury Lane Lodge No.2187, and Caernarvon Lodge No.708, meeting at Hampton Court, being honoured in 1889 with the appointment of Grand Superintendent of Works of the United Grand Lodge of England. The first edition of the Toynbee Record, in October 1888, states 'The singing classes are taught by Mr. W. Henry Thomas, the well-known composer of concert ballads.' Henry Thomas was a Captain in the 20th Middlesex, and there was no more famous composer of ballads at the time than Michael Maybrick. The pair became close friends, fellow members and Past Masters of Athenaeum Lodge No.1491. Maybrick joined the 20th Middlesex (Artists) Rifle Volunteers in 1886, lying about his age, giving it as 40 years old instead of 45. With a chest measurement of 41 inches, and height over 6 feet tall, he was an imposing presence, well-honed by an intensively active lifestyle.

The insignia on the helmet plate of the Artist Rifles represents Minerva, goddess of the arts, and Mars, god of War, inspiring the following little ditty, origin unknown, informally adopted by the regiment.   Could these strange lyrics have emanated from the mindset of the renowned balladeer Lieutenant Michael Maybrick?

Mars he was a God of War,
He didn't stop at trifles,
Minerva was a bloody whore,
So hence the Artists Rifles.

On the occasion of the inauguration of the new headquarters of the 20th Middlesex (Artists) Rifle Volunteers in Dukes Road, Euston, the opening ceremony was performed by their Royal Highnesses, the Prince and Princess of Wales, with vocal entertainment provided by Lieutenant Michael Maybrick, one of many occasions on which he would enjoy the company of the future King of England, Grand Master of the United Grand Lodge of England.

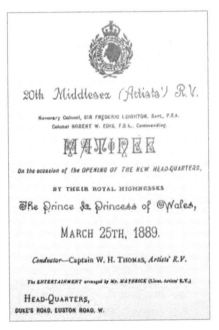

MARTHA TABRAM

Michael Maybrick, residing in Clarence Gate, Regents Park, had probably never heard of St. Jude's Church prior to joining the 20th Middlesex (Artists) Rifles Volunteers, but his Masonic colleague, Henry Thomas, would have wasted no time at all in proudly introducing him to the Reverend Samuel Barnett, at once delighted to

make the acquaintance of the renowned Mr. Michael Maybrick. Two years earlier in 1884, the poet Matthew Arnold had gifted to St. Jude's Church a large mosaic, which soon found pride of place over the fountain on the outside of the church, next to the entrance on Commercial Street. The mosaic, by Antonio Salviati, was entitled 'Time, Death and Judgement', from a painting by George Frederick Watts, widely considered the greatest painter of the

Victorian era, a close friend of Sir Frederic Leighton and the Rev. Samuel Barnett, and also responsible for a masterly interpretation of 'Orpheus and Eurydice', after whom Michael Maybrick had founded two Masonic Lodges. Within the church were displayed other graphic paintings by George F. Watts, similarly dark in content, with deeply metaphysical overtones.

On the right side of the entrance, and close to a beautifully modelled fountain, is a fine reproduction in mosaic of the well-known picture by G.F. Watts R.A., placed there to record the vicar's endeavour to make the lives of neighbours brighter by bringing them within the influence of beauty. Within the church one sees at once this has been done, for they are hung with pictures, the subjects of which are more accurately described as being serious and suggestive, than as common religious sense. There are for example, 'Love and Death', 'Death Crowning Innocence', and 'The Marriage

of Death.'

The Globe. September 1888.

Years later, Michael Maybrick's tombstone would bear the inscription, 'There Shall Be No More Death', an abnormal preoccupation with mortality which by now was deeply embedded in this increasingly disturbed psyche, eerily at ease with the necromantic images in and around St. Jude's Church. All that was missing was

the solace of the organ, his private retreat, his seat of meditation, an issue that was soon to be resolved. The Rev. Barnett would have been only too pleased to hand over a duplicate key of his humble church to the organ virtuoso Michael Maybrick. Just come and go as you please. Confidentiality assured, of course. This was destined to be his sanctuary. Taking his place at the organ, passions intensified in this surreal, macabre scenario, as stops were pulled and volume increased. Bach's Toccata and Fugue in D Minor, in flickering candlelight under the gaze of G.F. Watts's portentous images. Enigmatic as they were, further intrigue arose from the uncanny parallel of the church's location to his own St. Peter's, in Liverpool. On approaching the Whitechapel junction and turning left, in both cities the church is situated in the same location on the right-hand side. With the plans superimposed to scale, Maybrick's childhood Church Alley virtually runs through Toynbee Hall quadrangle, where the 20th Middlesex band

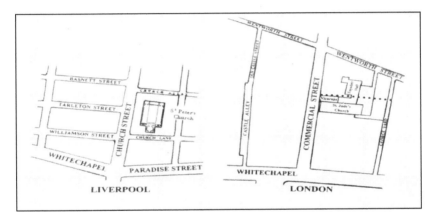

performed. Was his mind playing tricks? In the summer of 1888, the national celebrity returned to Liverpool, paying a visit to his beloved St. Peter's Church, evoking early memories of spiritual inspiration, followed by a mundane lunch break at the Post Office Tavern, still known to Michael Maybrick as 'The Poste House', where a pivotal decision was taken.

So be it, my mind is finally made. I took refreshment at the Poste House, it was there I finally decided London it shall be. And why not, is it not an ideal location? All who sell their dirty wares shall pay, of that I have no doubt. But shall I pay? I think not, I am too clever for that.   Diary of Jack the Ripper.

At the beginning of August 1888, Richard Mansfield was appearing on stage at the Lyceum Theatre, starring in Robert Louis Stevenson's 'Dr. Jekyll and Mr. Hyde', in which the respectable doctor mutates into alter-ego psychotic killer Mr. Hyde. The Daily Telegraph reported,

The most powerful and horrible thing that has ever been seen on the modern stage, would make any audience shudder and go home terrified in the dark watches of the night.

The Daily Telegraph. 1 August 1888.

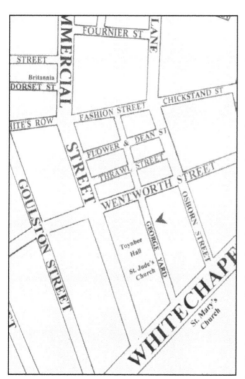

The theatre was full to capacity every night, terrifying audiences and soon becoming the talk of the town. On the 7th August 1888, the day after Bank Holiday Monday, there occurred the first of a series of events which would transpose the theatrical tale of Jekyll and Hyde onto the streets of Whitechapel, and horrify the entire nation. In George Yard, a lane just off Whitechapel, at 4.45 am, a lodger came across a figure curled up on the dark first floor landing of George Yard Building, Nothing unusual, except for the pool of blood alongside. Martha Tabram, known only as 'Emma' to the locals, despatched in a frenzy of multiple stab wounds. Constable

Thomas Barrett later testified,

I found the deceased laying on her back. I noticed the hands were clenched, but there was nothing in them. The clothes were turned up as far as the centre of her body, leaving the lower part of the body exposed. The legs were open, and altogether her position was such as to at once suggest in my mind that recent intimacy had taken place. East London Observer. 11 August 1888.

Her hands were lying by her side, clenched up. Her clothes were torn and completely disarranged, the bosom of the dress being torn away. She was in such a position as to infer that someone had been with her. Her clothes were thrown upwards. East London Advertiser. 11 August 1888.

George Yard is located immediately behind the rear wall of Toynbee Hall and St. Jude's Church. If the area plan of St. Peter's Church, Liverpool, were to be superimposed onto that of St. Jude's, Whitechapel, Church Alley would lead not only through the quadrangle of Toynbee Hall, where the 20th Middlesex band had been performing that weekend, but straight into George Yard Building. Was this another incredible coincidence, or the Machiavellian scheming of a demented soul, choosing location and then victim, less than fifty yards away from the jackal's lair in St. Jude's Church?

Six months previously, also over Bank Holiday, another Emma, Emma Smith, had been sexually assaulted and murdered in nearby Brick Lane. Violence dwelt hand in hand with poverty on the streets of Whitechapel, and that event had attracted only passive observation in the press, so why, after the murder of Martha Tabram, did someone consider it necessary to immediately form a Vigilance Association based at St. Jude's Church? Who was that someone, and was there an ulterior motive?

Toynbee Hall was in the heart of the terrorised area. One of the victims had been found within a few yards of the rear of the Settlement. The spot is still pointed out in a whisper to horrified visitors. The panic was amazing. In August, an Association was formed at St. Jude's, and the streets were patrolled by members of the Association, which included both residents and working men. The most important discovery was the deficiency of the police. The residents continued their patrols after their working men colleagues had given it up. They were, in fact, doing the work that should have been done by the police. Toynbee Hall. J.A.R. Pimlott.

So the residents of Toynbee Hall, and doubtless members of the Artists Rifle Regiment, worked the night shift once their local colleagues had gone home. Could our musician from the 20th Middlesex have been scheming more mischief, following his night-time encounter with Martha Tabram. Indeed, the suggestion of a Vigilance Association was nothing less than a stroke of genius. Just how the Whitechapel Murderer escaped detection has been a mystery awaiting a solution for well over a century. The creation of a Vigilance Association not only provided street-credibility in otherwise unfamiliar territory, but to the fearful women of Whitechapel it offered re-assurance and protection. To the killer it was a cloak of invisibility, and what better way to explore the area than by nightly guided tours, accompanied by a street reared local, familiar from childhood with the maze of alleyways linking the back streets, one seeking an assassin who would never be caught, the other silently mapping the area and plotting murder with military precision, at the same time targeting and gaining the confidence of potential victims. Add to this the bonus of meeting bobbies on the beat and learning their rotas, which, as endorsed by police diary notes at later crime scenes, were undertaken on specific routes to a precise timetable. Windows of opportunity, with the cold eyes of a killer peering in.

The victim, Martha Tabram, a known prostitute, was 39 years old, 5' 3" in height, with brown hair worn in a bun. Martha's companion for most of Bank Holiday weekend, and with her earlier on the night of murder, was known locally as Pearly Poll, who knew the victim not as Martha, only by her street name Emma, which would delay formal identification of the body until the 16th August.

The Metropolitan Police report reads as follows,

I beg to report that the body of the woman found murdered in George Yard Buildings on 7th inst. has been identified by Henry Samuel Tabram of 6 River Terrace, East Greenwich, as that of his wife, who left him some years ago. She also has been identified by Mrs. Luckhurst of 4 Star Place, Commercial Road, as her lodger, Mrs. Tabram, but passing by the name of Turner, taking the name of a man with whom she lived until a month ago. Inquiries have also been made, and it is found that the deceased resided at 19 George Street, (a common lodging house) and passed there in the name of 'Emma'.

The inquest on the unidentified body was opened on the 9th August, under Deputy Coroner George Collier, with medical evidence provided by Dr. Timothy Killeen.

On examining the body externally, I found no less than thirty-nine puncture wounds. The lower part of the body was penetrated in one place, the wound being three inches in length, and one in depth. From appearances, there was no reason to suppose that recent intimacy had taken place. I do not think that all the wounds were inflicted by the same instrument, because there was one wound on the breast bone which did not correspond with the other wounds on the body, which would probably have been inflicted with some form of dagger. There was no sign whatsoever of any struggle having taken place, and there was a great deal of blood between the legs, which were separated.

East London Observer. 11 August 1888.

The doctor differentiates between the thirty-nine external

puncture wounds and the discreetly phrased lower penetration, which, coupled with the large volume of blood between the legs, bears a marked similarity to the treatment meted out to Emma Smith six months earlier. The doctor further states the puncture in the chest must have been made by 'some form of dagger.' Could the instrument have been a sword-stick, or was it a bayonet as worn on the belt of every 20th Middlesex (Artists) Rifle Volunteer?

The Toynbee Journal of February 1889 advises, *'Last summer, several concerts were given in the quad, with enthusiastic audiences of three or four hundred.'*

Almost certainly, concerts would

have been performed on Bank Holiday Mondays, placing the band of the 20th Middlesex (Artists) Rifle Volunteers, including baritone vocalist Lieutenant Michael Maybrick, firmly in Toynbee Hall on the dates of both murders.

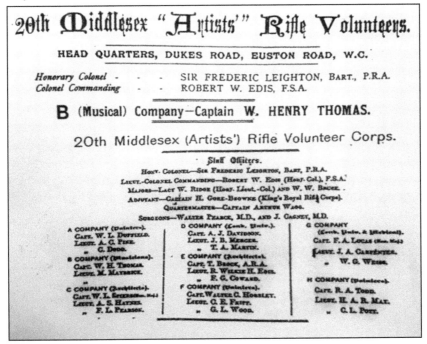

The mystery surrounding the murder in George Yard Court, Whitechapel, has not been cleared up. The woman, it may be remembered, was found brutally murdered, no fewer than about thirty stabs having been inflicted on her body. It was thought that the wounds were inflicted with a bayonet, and that the murderer must have been a soldier. The soldiers in several barracks have been paraded before the police and witnesses, but with no result. The Star. 24 August 1888.

Evidence concerning the soldiers had emanated mainly from Pearly Poll, considered by the police to be an unreliable witness.

Soldiers were interviewed without any outcome at the Tower of London and Wellington Barracks, but there is no record of any such investigation concerning the 20th Middlesex (Artists) Rifle Volunteers, some of whom would have been performing that very night in Toynbee Hall, less than one hundred yards away from the crime scene.

EMMA SMITH

Only after Martha Tabram's gruesome murder did the press collectively consider the death of Emma Smith, some six months earlier, as the work of the same killer, despite at the time having attracted scant interest.   Emma Smith was a 45 year old prostitute, 5'2" in height with brown hair, a heavy drinker when finances allowed, and known to be confrontational.   At 6.00 pm on Bank Holiday Monday, 3rd April 1888, Emma left her lodgings to tout for business, and, at just after 4.00 am the following morning, staggered into her lodging house at 18 George Street, using a shawl to stem heavy bleeding from a deep wound to her private parts, evidently caused by a blunt object, probably a walking stick.   Emma also had severe head injuries, and one ear had been partially torn off.

Emma's initial story, relayed by one of her friends, was that around 1.30 am on Tuesday, 4th April, the day after the Bank Holiday Monday, she had been attacked and robbed by a gang of two or three men in Brick Lane, off Whitechapel Road, returning to her lodging house at around 4.00 am, a long delay, considering the blood loss caused by the severity of her wounds.   The manager, Mary Russell, left the house unattended, at risk of losing her job, to escort Emma to the London Hospital, accompanied by one of the doss-house residents, Annie Lee. It was a long walk to the hospital, passing through the area where the assault took place, with no attempt being made by Mary Russell to alert the police. Clearly, Emma Smith had no idea that she was going to die, as the bleeding was apparently stemmed at the hospital, but peritonitis set in, and Emma died painfully later that morning. Not until Emma Smith's inquest, three days later, on the 7th April, were the police notified and an investigation instigated. The police reports on the incident read as follows,

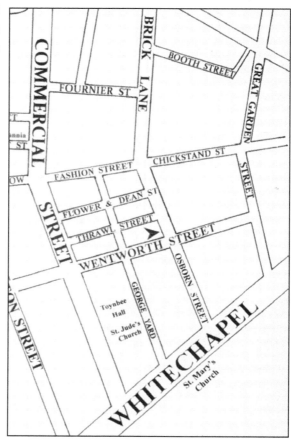

The first the police knew of this attack was from the Coroner's Office, who reported in the usual manner on the 6th inst. None of the P.C.'s in the area had heard or seen anything at all, and the streets were said to be quiet at that time. The offence had been committed on the pathway opposite No. 10, Brick Lane, about 100 yards from George Street, and half a mile from the London Hospital to which the deceased walked. She would have passed a number of P.C.'s en route, but none was informed of the incident, or asked to render assistance. The peritoneum had been penetrated by a blunt instrument thrust up the woman's passage, and peritonitis had set in, which caused death. She was aged 45 years, 5 feet 2 inches high, complexion fair, hair light brown, scar on right temple. No description of the men.

Insp. Edmund Reid.

Head was bruised. Right ear torn, rupture of peritoneum.

According to the deceased the motive was robbery. Deceased could not describe the men who had ill-used her, but said there was three of them, and she was attacked about 1.30 am on the 3rd, while passing Whitechapel Church. Witness Mary Russell, deputy at 18 George Street, Spitalfields, Annie Lee, lodger (these two escorted her to London Hospital) George Haslip and Margaret Hames, (lodger at the above address who was last to see her alive.) Witnesses said they did not think it necessary to report the circumstances to the police. Whole of police on duty deny all knowledge of the occurrence. Inspector John West.

Witness George Haslip was the doctor on duty at the hospital, aged 24, and only recently out of medical school. Fellow lodger and close friend Margaret Hames did not accompany Emma to hospital, but was there by her side when she died. In the same profession, Margaret had experienced a very similar encounter with an unknown assailant four months earlier, on the 8th December 1887, when hospital records held at the London Metropolitan Archives confirm that Margaret was admitted suffering from facial and chest injuries, so severe that she was detained until the 26th December. Had Margaret been traumatised into silence that night by threats from her assailant, and did she warn Emma before her hospital admission against giving a description of the man? The pair had to survive alone on the streets of Whitechapel in the dead of night, the man was still out there, and squealing to the police would get them into a lot of trouble. Say nothing Emma.

The police statements indicate that Emma had been assaulted on two separate occasions, early in the morning of 4th April, 1888. In Inspector Reid's account, the assault took place outside No.10 Brick Lane, so precise a description of the location that it must be deemed accurate. In Inspector West's account, an assault by three men took place whilst passing St. Mary's Church, known locally as Whitechapel Church, over 150 yards away on Whitechapel High Street. The police were unaware of the incidents until the inquest three days after Emma's death, so the separate statements must have emanated from the named witnesses, Mary Russell and Margaret Hames.   Logically, it would appear that Emma had been robbed and bruised by three men near St. Mary's Church at around 1.30 am, but had continued to tout for business, in order to recoup her losses.   Later, at around 4.00 am in Brick Lane, Emma encountered the assailant who inflicted the serious wounds, following which she staggered home and was accompanied to hospital, traumatised and terrified of incurring retribution from the assailant, hence the deliberate avoidance of police involvement on the night.   At the time of admission Emma was either unable or unwilling to give her name, and may only have been positively identified at the inquest, inferring that initial information on identity was withheld by those accompanying her to the London Hospital.   This 'want of identity' is confirmed by Dr. George Haslip, probably the first person to link this murder to that of Martha 'Emma' Tabram five months later, and certainly the most qualified to make such an assertion.

Want of identity was painfully apparent in the horrible murder of the woman in Whitechapel some months ago, when precisely similar injuries were inflicted as in the present case.   Dr. Haslip stated to our reporter that most fiendish brutality had been used in this case, and there seems to be very little question that both murders were committed by the same person.

Evening News. 6 September 1888.

Here is first hand and totally reliable evidence that Martha Tabram was sexually wounded in the same manner as Emma Smith, a fact overlooked in most other contemporary critiques. The weapon used to cause Martha's deep chest injury was not the same as that which caused the four inch cut or tear in her private parts, but rather a walking stick once again, causing what Dr. Haslip determined to be a 'precisely similar injury' to that incurred by Emma Smith. Others were of similar opinion to Dr. Haslip, including elements of the press, and officers at Scotland Yard.

The circumstances of the outrage are at present as mysterious as those connected with the brutal and yet undiscovered murder perpetrated a few months ago, also in Whitechapel, where some miscreant, in the dead of night, murdered a woman in the street by thrusting a walking stick or other blunt instrument into her body with great violence. For ferocity, the two cases are somewhat analogous, and some of the Scotland Yard experts in tracing criminals and forthcoming crime incline to the opinion that one man is responsible for the two crimes.
The Echo. 10 August 1888.

Yet more events were to unfold, as earlier that same April evening, local prostitute Malvina Hayes had been stretchered into the same London Hospital as Emma Smith, unconscious, and also with serious head injuries. The police attended at the hospital, and their availability within the building at the same time as Emma Smith further endorses Emma's reluctance to involve the police. The wounds inflicted on Malvina earlier on the same night indicate the very real possibility, or even likelihood, that both assaults had been perpetrated by the same man.

Malvina Hayes, who received very serious injuries to her head and scalp on the night of the Bank Holiday, has been from that time until Tuesday quite unconscious in the London Hospital, no sounds but moans having escaped her lips. The sufferer has been under the care of Mr. George E. Haslip, the house surgeon, and yesterday the patient, on regaining consciousness, was only able to briefly relate the circumstances of the outrage. On many

points her memory is an entire blank, and when questioned as to what her assailant was like, she replied, 'I cannot remember, my mind is gone.' The hospital authorities at once communicated with Detective Sergeant William New, who has charge of the case, and certain information which casually passed through the woman's lips may perhaps lead to a clue respecting the would be murderer.
Eastern Post & City Chronicle. 14 April 1888.

ANOTHER OUTRAGE AT WHITECHAPEL

THE VICTIM A WEEK UNCONSCIOUS.

Whitechapel is becoming notorious for acts of brutal violence against women in the streets, and to-day inquiries are being pursued with reference to an attempted murder which occurred as far back as Monday night last, though the victim, who is still lying at the London Hospital, has not yet regained consciousness, and has, therefore, been unable to give any description of her assailant, It appears that on the night in question loud screams were heard in the vicinity of the railway arch adjoining the Leman-street Station, and a lodging-house keeper residing in Wellclose-square saw a man treating a woman with great violence. An alarm was raised, but the assailant ran away, leaving the woman lying moaning in the roadway. She was immediately conveyed to the London Hospital, where she was afterwards identified as Malvina Haynes, a married woman, residing at 29, Newman-street, Whitechapel. Up to this afternoon she had not sufficiently recovered to make any intelligible statement as to how she met with her injuries, which are principally confined to her head. It is, indeed, very DOUBTFUL WHETHER SHE WILL RECOVER from the murderous attack, as the concussion of the brain, from which Mrs. Haynes has chiefly suffered, is of so dangerous a character that the medical staff at the London Hospital think that recovery is a matter of great uncertainty. Inspector Reid and Detective-Sergeant William New are using every endeavour to trace the assailant, but at present no apprehension has been made.

The Echo. 9 April 1888.

Five months later, following the murder of Martha Tabram, the death of Emma Smith would come to be regarded by the London press as the first of the Whitechapel Murders, which, coupled with that of Martha Tabram, would come to be known as the Bank Holiday Murders. Emma Smith and Martha 'Emma' Tabram lived in lodgings only yards away from each other at 18 and 19 George Street, and were the same age, with similar physical characteristics. Was this a coincidence, could there have been a case of mistaken identity, or did both unlock the traumatic memory of a similar Emma, many years ago in Liverpool? Four days after the latest atrocity, an article appeared in the Star, containing a startlingly astute observation, which went totally ignored.

On Bank Holidays, our hypothetical murderer would not be in workaday clothes or have his tools about him, but he would be armed with a stick, which is part of the holiday paraphernalia, or with a bayonet supposing he were a Volunteer, and in the early hours of the morning after Bank Holiday he would be in the immediate vicinity of his workshop. The victims were killed on the mornings after Bank Holidays. One was wounded with a stick, and the other with some weapon like a bayonet. Question for the police or public. Is there a slaughterman or a knacker living in Whitechapel who cannot account for his whereabouts on the morning after these murders, or is he in the Volunteers, or has a pal in the Volunteers who is given to heavy drinking?

The Star. 11 September 1888.

Michael Maybrick had joined the 20th Middlesex (Artists) Rifle Volunteers in 1886, and was a regular attendee at Toynbee Hall. The assault on Margaret Hames had taken place in December 1887, followed by increasingly vicious attacks in April 1888 on Malvina Hayes and Emma Smith, who died as the result of her wounds. The choice of victim and location, within a short walking distance of Toynbee Hall, may have been deliberate, but was murder initially on the agenda? In this Shadowland environment where prostitution was rife, Michael Maybrick was beginning to exhibit the delusionary symptoms of psychopathic schizophrenia, but he was not yet a purposeful killer. Had the voices instructed him to punish or to kill? Maybrick's physical description had not been provided by

Malvina Hayes to the police in December, and he was not a wanted man as such, so perhaps he had set out that April night with similar intent in mind, only to find himself drawn into an uncontrollable sequence of events, resulting in the death of Emma Smith. That had been the point of no return, and five months later, after a similar concert on Bank Holiday Monday in August, Martha 'Emma' Tabram's death had been carefully planned, and was so very enjoyable. Eighty years later, Peter Sutcliffe, the Yorkshire Ripper, fellow patron of the Museum of Anatomy, provides a chilling insight into the mind of a serial killer at the outset of his descent into depravity.

That was the incident that started it off. I suddenly felt seething with rage. I hit her once or twice on the head and she fell down on her back. I knew I had gone too far. I thought that to make certain she was dead I would stab her in places like the lungs and the throat. Before I stabbed her I pulled her blouse or whatever it was so I could see where I was stabbing her. I was in a blind panic when I was stabbing her just to make sure she wouldn't tell anyone. That was the turning point. The next one I remember there was an overpowering smell of cheap perfume and sweat, this served all the more for me to hate this woman even though I didn't know her. She had an overcoat on, she was heavily built and had brown hair. Looking back I can see how the first murder had unhinged me completely. I wanted to do what I had got in mind as soon as possible. I hit her over the head with the hammer. I think I hit her twice. I then made sure she was dead in order to satisfy some sort of sexual revenge on her. I stabbed her frenziedly without thought all over her body. I was seething with hate for her. I remember picking up a piece of wood about two feet long and pushing up against her vagina with it as she lay on her back. I had a feeling of satisfaction and justification for what I'd done.

Confession Statement of Peter Sutcliffe, 'The Yorkshire Ripper'.

SIR CHARLES WARREN

Twenty years earlier and two thousand miles away, members of the British funded Palestine Expeditionary Fund had been busy excavating around and underneath ancient Jerusalem, with particular attention focused on the Temple Mount. Foremost of those intrepid explorers was Captain Charles Warren of the Royal Engineers, whose dual interest was to prove the existence of the legendary city of Solomon, and its association with Freemasonry. Warren's Masonic career had begun in 1859,

SIR CHARLES WARREN.

when he was initiated into the Royal Lodge of Friendship in Gibraltar. Whilst in Jerusalem, then controlled and zealously guarded by the Muslim Caliphate, Warren instigated, at great personal risk, a Masonic Lodge meeting in a subterranean cavern beneath the Temple Mount, in which he consecrated the Reclamation Lodge of Jerusalem. This was followed by a further Lodge meeting in a cavern within the deep quarries beneath north Jerusalem, close to the Damascus Gate, where legend had it Solomon's masons quarried stone for the first temple. Now known as Zedekiah's Cave, the cavern has subsequently been used for lodge meetings on rare occasions over the years.

There was little that Charles Warren did not know about biblical Jerusalem, leaving the important legacy of his excavations in 'Warren's Shaft', tunnelled beneath the walls of the ancient city, dating back to the age of the kings of Judea, and ranking high in the list of Victorian archaeological discoveries, earning him the sobriquet 'Jerusalem Warren'. Following military service in South Africa, and promotion in Bechuanaland to the rank of Lieutenant Colonel, he was knighted in 1883, and one year later was elected a Fellow of the Royal Society. On returning to England in 1886, Sir Charles Warren was appointed Commissioner of the Metropolitan Police, a position which, following events in Whitechapel two years later, would leave him wishing he had never left the army.

Two years prior to leaving for Bechuanaland, Warren had set in motion the formalities for the creation of a new Masonic Lodge in London. On his return to England in 1886, the Quatuor Coronati Lodge No.2076 was consecrated, and Sir Charles Warren, one of the twelve founder members, was elected as first Worshipful Master. This was a Lodge of exclusive membership, dedicated to the research and understanding of Masonic history and associated archaeology. The lectures make very heavy, almost mind-numbing reading, one of those slightly less so being 'On the Orientation of the Temples', composed by Sir Charles Warren, and recounted to the Lodge members in March 1887, included in which is one notable phrase , 'The key to the whole subject may be found in the book of Ezekiel.' Sir Charles Warren knew the book word for word, and before long those words would take on a profoundly different significance.

Membership of Quatuor Coronati Lodge was rigidly restricted, but within twelve months a system of correspondence membership was adopted, without entailing actual admission to Lodge meetings. Initially, the total number of applicants would be announced in the quarterly minutes, approved and accepted, but in 1888 only the number of actual acceptances was noted, inferring a number of informal rejections, hardly surprising given the extremely high standard of Masonic knowledge demanded by the core members.

The renowned Michael Maybrick would doubtless have considered himself worthy, even entitled to membership of this august group, affording an unmissable opportunity both to gain kudos and to expand his knowledge of Jerusalem in a Masonic context. What then if such an approach had been made, with uncharacteristic humility, by Brother Michael Maybrick to Brother Sir Charles Warren, perhaps in the Savage Club, only to be met with a polite, even patronising rejection. If this did indeed occur, the Commissioner of the Metropolitan Police would have been blissfully unaware that he would soon find himself on very shaky ground indeed. The psychopathic ego of Michael Maybrick would have been grievously offended. Within Freemasonry, Sir Charles Warren held the rank of Past Grand Senior Deacon, and occupied high office in more than one Order.

There follows an illustration depicting Sir Charles Warren on the lower right, at an installation ceremony of HRH The Prince of Wales, in the company of Prince Albert Victor, the Earl of Lathom, the Duke of York, and the Bishop of St. Alban's, admirably encapsulated by author Bruce Robinson.

All were members of a self-regulating matrix, in which everyone knew everyone, and everyone knew in what direction the bowing was done.   Bruce Robinson. They All Love Jack.

The Commissioner of Metropolitan Police was very well connected indeed, not only in the hierarchy of Freemasonry, but in the higher echelons of London society. Within the force itself, however, resentment was simmering over Warren's military approach to policing, which was to manifest itself publicly during his first year in office. Irish independence was a matter of national concern, prompting numerous debates in Parliament, and with sections of the public determined to impose their opinions on the subject. A peaceful protest was officially arranged for the 13th November 1887 in Trafalgar Square, but Sir Charles Warren, with the tact and diplomacy honed by suppressing natives in Africa, promptly issued an ultimatum prohibiting the meeting, and when the day arrived, immediately sent in the police, aided by armed military. In the ensuing confrontation, known as 'Bloody Sunday', fifty people ended up in hospital, and three in prison. Sir Charles Warren's unpopularity with both press and public was assured.

SERIOUS RIOTING in TRAFALGAR · SQUARE. THE MILITARY AND POLICE ATTACK THE MOB.

MARY ANN NICHOLS

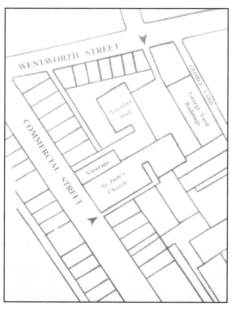

Royalties from a succession of ballads ensured a regular source of income for the flamboyant baritone Michael Maybrick, affording him a fine residence overlooking Regent's Park, and a retreat on the Isle of Wight, whilst enhancing his fame with a continuous succession of stage performances, fuelling his insatiable ego. However, the glory of the limelight soon succumbed to the allure of the shadows, and during August 1888, there was ample time for evening patrols with the St. Jude's Vigilance Association, allowing him to blend into the community, gaining the confidence of his future victims, then retreating to his religious safe house.

By this time the modus operandi had been well rehearsed, and ventures would be conducted by way of the common rear exit from St. Jude's Church and Toynbee Hall, served by a gated passageway into Wentworth Street, allowing access for discreet comings and goings at night.

The interest in the poor was not confined to mere sentimental sighing. Being Victorians, albeit rich and class conscious, they did something to show their sincerity in a practical way. They put the hat around, and with the money raised they built those settlements in the East End which exist to this day. Perhaps the most famous of these is Toynbee Hall, which adjoins St. Jude's Church in Commercial Street, where the presence of a 'toff' would not only be noticeable, but, to be expected. Like Toynbee Hall, its back doors also provided easy access to any of the dark yards of Whitechapel.   Michael Harrison. Clarence.

Early in the morning of Friday the 30th August, Mary Ann Nichols was refused lodgings for not having the money to pay for a bed. Four pence was all it cost, but by 1.30 am, Mary was penniless and out on the streets. Two hours later her dead body was found in a pool of blood by a pair of cart drivers in Buck's Row, off Brady Street, close to the London Hospital in Whitechapel High Street. One of them alerted a policeman some distance away, and on return found another policeman, P.C. John Thain, already at the murder scene, which he had passed exactly thirty minutes earlier, confirming the street empty at that time. Mary Ann Nichols was the killer's first victim as a Whitechapel vigilante, and, in the course of his patrols, P.C. Thain's routine had been diligently monitored over the previous few days, with twenty five clear minutes carefully timed and logged. Timing was crucial, two lives were at stake, the victim's, and most importantly, that of the killer. With the trusting Mary Ann by his side, the pair were less than thirty seconds behind the beat bobby, listening to the sound of his boots clumping off into the night, then sidestep into the gate entrance, followed instantly by the deadly 20th Middlesex rear choke lock. Out with the knife, and down to business.

Between three and four in the morning, the body of a murdered woman was found lying in the gutter in Buck's Row. It presented a horrible spectacle. The throat had been cut from ear to ear, tracing from left to right. The wound was two inches wide, and blood was flowing profusely. She was immediately conveyed to the Whitechapel Mortuary, where it was found that besides the wound in the throat, the lower part of the abdomen was completely ripped open, with the bowels protruding. The wound extended nearly to her breast, and must have been effected with a large knife. The body was warm when discovered. The brutality of the murder is beyond conception and beyond description. The throat was cut in two gashes, the instrument having been a sharp one, used in a most ferocious and reckless way. The knife was jabbed into the deceased at the lower part of the abdomen, and then drawn upwards twice. Lloyds Weekly Newspaper. 2 September 1888.

On the day following the Nichols murder, mother and daughter Caroline and Charlotte Colville, living in adjoining Brady Street, related what they had heard early that morning. Eleven year old Charlotte began,

Early this morning, before it was light, I heard terrible cries of 'Murder! Murder! Police! Police! Murder! Murder!' They seemed a good way down Brady Street to the right where the marks of bloody hands were. Then the sound came up the street towards our house, and I heard a scuffling and bumping against our shutters. I got out of bed and woke my mother. The woman kept calling 'Murder! Police!' and the sounds went on in the direction of Buck's Row. I am sure the first sounds seemed to come from where the bloodstains of hands are on the wall.
. Lloyds Weekly News. 2 September 1888.

Mrs. Colville added that her daughter woke her with the news that a woman was trying to break into their house, and heard with her own ears a woman screaming 'Murder! Police!' five or six times, alongside the steps of a single person. Unfortunately, there is no indication of the time when this incident occurred. Before the introduction of the Summertime Act in 1916, sunset on the 29th August was around 7.00 pm An eleven year old child went to bed, fell asleep, was woken up by noises in the dark, woke her mother, and the pair witnessed the sounds. This could have been any time of night, following which the assailant would have had time to assess the situation and monitor any resultant police activity, which in this case appears to have been totally absent. The incident must, however, have occurred before the discovery of Mary Ann's body at 3.00 am, following which the area was a hive of police activity. Mrs. Colville and her daughter lived in Brady Street, where Charlotte describes 'bloodstains of hands on the wall'. It is important to note that no bloodstains were found on any walls in Buck's Row.

Brady Street is a long thoroughfare that runs to the bottom of Buck's Row. Early on Friday morning, fresh blood stains were

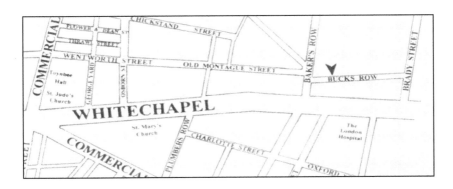

observed for quite a distance along the side-walks. There would be drop after drop every two or three feet, and sometimes six feet apart for a distance, and then a larger pool and a splash. As soon as the murder came known, a lively interest was taken in these blood stains, and they began to be traced. They were soon found to be on either side of the street, and it was afterwards seen that the bleeding person had travelled, or had been carried in a zigzag line. The trail was easily followed down Brady Street for 150 yards to Honey's Mews. In front of the gateway there was a large stain, looking as if the bleeding person had fallen against the wall and then lain there. From here to the foot of Buck's

Row, in which the body was found, the trail of blood was clearly marked. The zig-zag direction it took, crossing and re-crossing the street, was, and is, a matter of mystery.

Lloyds Weekly News. 2 September 1888.

The 'foot of Buck's Row' refers to the junction of Brady Street and Buck's Row, with no inference that the blood trail entered Buck's Row. Close on-site investigation confirmed for certain that Mary Ann Nichols had been killed where the body was found, in a contained pool of blood, and had definitely not zig-zagged along Brady Street, leaving a trail of blood on the pavement, and blood stains on the wall. Three slaughtermen, operating all night in a yard off Buck's Row, were emphatic that they had heard nothing unusual nearby, and after a grilling from the police, were discounted as potential suspects. All indications pointed to the unlikely scenario of a separate assault having taken place earlier that night in Brady Street, out of hearing range of the slaughterhouse. There had been a bloodthirsty maniac on the prowl, electrically charged with the need to kill one carefully selected victim, but feeling the compulsion to attack someone else he had unintentionally encountered prior to the planned event. There was only one body. The other injured party had disappeared. A statement was issued by Inspector Helson.

The report that bloodstains were found leading from Brady Street to Buck's Row was not true ... neither bloodstains nor wheel marks were found to indicate that the body had been deposited where found. . Daily News. 1 September 1888.

The statement is misleading, but not intentionally so. Had Inspector Helson stated 'into Buck's Row', instead of 'to Buck's Row' it would have made perfect sense, and such was the intent. The Inspector was at odds to point out that the body had most definitely not been deposited in Buck's Row, neither did the blood trail in Brady Street lead to the body.   There must have been two separate incidents on the same night, the first having taken place whilst the assailant waited for his specially selected victim, Mary Ann Nichols, singled out well before that night as part of a pre-determined sequence of events.   The Brady Street victim simply wasn't part of the plan, but, in the course of conversation, something had triggered a spontaneous reaction in the psychopath's head.   This woman was severely assaulted, but allowed to live, terrified out of her mind by the threat of death were anyone to be told of the event, let alone provide details of the assailant.   So who was this other victim, and why was she allowed to live?

On Sunday the 1st September, a woman named Margaret Millous was signed into the London Hospital, just across Whitechapel High Street from Brady Street, for emergency surgery listed as a 'wound of radial artery located in the forearm', a wound typically sustained when raising the arm in self-defence.   That in itself is a serious injury, but indications are that further injuries may well have been sustained, as Margaret was detained in hospital for sixteen days until the 17th September.   No reference to the event was made in the British press, but over in America the following article appeared on the 31st August, 1888, the day after the murder of Mary Ann Nichols.

The police were called to a house in Whitechapel last night on an alarm of murder, in which they found a woman in great suffering. On examination it was found she had been horribly and indecently assaulted.   She could not tell who had inflicted the wounds, save that he was a tall man with a black beard.   The woman was taken to a hospital, and it is doubtful whether she can recover from her terrible injuries.   This is the third of the kind known to the police.   It is believed the awful work is the crime of one man and he is a maniac.   Illinois Daily Reporter. 31 August 1888.

.

This article, appearing four thousand miles away on the far side of the Atlantic, has considerably more bearing on the Whitechapel murders than appears at first sight.   Why, for instance, would the assailant allow a clearly incapacitated victim to escape, albeit terrified and numbed into silence?   The murderer was already on a specific mission to kill Mary Ann Nichols, according to a pre-determined plan, when he encountered Margaret Millous who, for whatever reason, sparked a psychotic reaction, resulting in a 'horrible and indecent' assault, uncannily reminiscent of the incident involving Malvina Hayes, attacked and injured prior to the penetrative sexual assault and resultant death of Emma Smith in Brick Lane, six months earlier.   Did the names upset the murderer?   Strange as it may seem, this may have been exactly the case.   A pattern was evolving.

Malvina Hayes
Martha Tabram
Margaret Millous
Mary Ann Nichols

Within the safe confines of the London Hospital, the police had a potential witness capable of identifying the assailant, very possibly the killer of Mary Ann Nichols.   Margaret Millous had suffered her suppurating wounds for over twenty-four hours, before an unnamed third party alerted the police to her deteriorating condition, and she was duly taken to hospital, on the 30th or the 31st August, prior to the article in the Illinois Reporter, which referred to the hospital admission.   The third party had evidently provided details to a newly arrived American journalist, who duly telegraphed the scoop back to his base in Illinois, a financial inducement possibly easing the arrangement.

Feverish, in pain, and with emotions in turmoil, having narrowly escaped death at the hands of a crazed knife-wielding psychopath, the last thing Margaret needed was to be named as a potential eye-witness and informant.   Terrified out of her wits, she may well have been unable to speak coherently, but one day later, after her admission, once safe and secure in her hospital bed, she gave her name, and was duly logged in on the 1st September. This would tally with the newspaper report being dated the 31st August, the day before Margaret Millous's official admission to the London Hospital.

Interestingly, the Illinois Daily Reporter refers to the attack as being 'the third of the kind known to the police', referring to the previous murders of Emma Smith and Martha Tabram, and indicating that this report was communicated prior to reports filtering through on the murder of Mary Ann Nichols.   The article really was hot off the press, and exclusive.   In other American newspapers, including the New York Times, news of the Nichols murder did not headline until the following day, with no reference to the Millous incident.   This was indeed a one-off scoop for the overseas correspondent of the Illinois Daily Reporter, copied one day later in the 'Logansport News,' in the neighbouring state of Indiana, but nowhere else. No mention was made either in the British press of Margaret Millous's admission to hospital, and the matter soon faded into obscurity.   Seemingly the police were following their own agenda, intent on keeping the Brady Street incident, together with their witness, under wraps.

The matter was being dealt with by Inspector Frederick Abberline, a seasoned Whitechapel policeman with over fourteen years' experience, promoted into Scotland Yard nine months previously, but drafted back to Whitechapel 'H' Division to supervise the investigation, and so far as he was concerned, the less the press knew the better. The police were silent at the time, but the following carefully worded report appeared in Lloyd's Weekly a month after the event, obtusely confirming, but at the same time sidelining the incident, adding false information to disguise the real facts and reassure the killer, thus safeguarding the life of a very valuable potential witness.

An alarming story was told to a detective yesterday, and it is understood that the Metropolitan Police have for some time been cognisant of its details. If this statement be true, and there appears to be no reason to question it, then sometime between the date of the Hanbury Street murder and last Sunday, the bloodthirsty maniac who is now terrifying Whitechapel, unsuccessfully attempted another outrage. The woman who so narrowly escaped death is married, but admits having entered into conversation with a strange man for an immoral purpose. She alleges that he tripped her up, so that she fell upon the pavement. He made an effort to cut her throat, but she shielded herself with her arm, and in doing so received a cut upon it. Alarmed by his failure, and fearing her shrieks, the would be murderer ran off, and the woman, when discovered, was removed to the hospital. She has since been discharged, and the wound on her arm is still to be seen. The occurrence is said to have occurred ten days ago, in a bye turning off Commercial Street. Unfortunately, the woman was so much in liquor when she was assaulted that she cannot recollect the man's face or dress, and has been unable to give a description of him, which may account for the secrecy which has been maintained in regard to her attack. Daily Telegraph. 3 October 1888.

Secrecy? Cognisant of the details for some time? Definitely. Off Commercial Street? Definitely not, and no mention of the 'horrible and indecent' sexual assault. The shrieks, however, had been definitely confirmed by Caroline and Charlotte Colville. A carefully contrived account bearing elements of truth and deliberate inaccuracies, relayed to the press by a certain detective. The press had their story, the matter was closed, and the witness's apparent loss of memory would serve to deter the murderer from retribution. Top marks to Inspector Abberline, who now had his covert sights on a 'tall man with a beard', knowing full well that the beard was as real as the story he had fed to the press.

Mary Ann Nichols' throat had been cut from ear to ear, with the lower part of her abdomen   stabbed and ripped open with greater intensity than inflicted on Martha Tabram.   There was an impression of a ring having been worn on one finger, but no trace of it was found.   Mary Ann Nichols was 5 feet 2 inches in height, 44 years old, with brown eyes, dark complexion, and brown hair turning grey, with five missing front teeth.   Unsurprisingly, the autopsy did not reveal any evidence of sexual intercourse.

The body is that of a person in poor circumstances, and her appearance was borne out by the mark 'Lambeth Workhouse P.R.', found on the petticoat bands.   A woman named Mary Ann Monk, at present an inmate of Lambeth Workhouse, was taken to the mortuary, and identified the body as that of Mary Ann Nichols.   They were inmates of that workhouse together in April and May last, the deceased having been passed on there by another workhouse.   The Echo. 1 September 1888.

Whilst undoubtedly a pitiable character, Mary Ann Nichols was no shrinking violet, a dissolute alcoholic, given to sleeping rough if needs be, and not shy of stealing.   On the occasion of her arrest in Trafalgar Square twelve months earlier, the press reported,

Nichols was stated to be the worst woman on the Square, and at

the police station was very disorderly.

Evening Standard. 6 October 1887.

Panic spread throughout Whitechapel. Police patrols were stepped up, and women remained indoors during the hours of darkness, except for those whose very survival depended on a equal underclass of males, trading coppers for sexual gratification. The streets were for the most part deserted, women fearful for their lives, and men fearful of being taken for the murderer. Then four days later, came a breakthrough. The word was out in Whitechapel that a man had been threatening prostitutes over the previous few weeks, described as between thirty and forty years old, 5 feet 4 inches in height, with black hair, thick neck, small eyes, and an evil grin, a carbon copy of Dr. Jekyll's alter ego. As the search spread, the press seized on the name by which he was known in the neighbourhood, 'Leather Apron'.

People wish to know why the police do not arrest 'Leather Apron'. If, as many of the people suspect, he is the real author of the three murders which, in everybody's judgment, were done by the same person, he is a more ghoulish and devilish brute than can be found on all of the pages of shocking fiction. He has kicked, injured, bruised and terrified a hundred of them already to testify to the outrages. He carries a razor-like knife, and two weeks ago, drew it on a woman called 'Widow Annie', threatening at the same time with his malignant grin and ugly eyes to 'rip her up.' The Star, London. 5 September 1888.

The widespread paranoia could easily have resulted in the public lynching of 'Leather Apron', had the police not traced him first, the arrest being made by an astute local bobby, Sergeant Thicke. John Pizer, maker of leather slippers, was duly detained in Leman Street Police Station, where it was officially established, after a few days incarceration, mainly for his own safety, that the apron

GHASTLY MURDER

IN THE EAST-END.
DREADFUL MUTILATION OF A WOMAN.

Capture : Leather Apron

Another murder of a character even more diabolical than that perpetrated in Buck's Row, on Friday week, was discovered in the same neighbourhood, on Saturday morning. At about six o'clock a woman was found lying in a back yard at the foot of a passage leading to a lodging-house in Old Brown's Lane, Spitalfields. The house is occupied by a Mrs. Richardson, who lets it out to lodgers, and the door which admits to this passage, at the foot of which lies the yard where the body was found, is always open for the convenience of lodgers. A lodger named Davis was going down to work at the time mentioned and found the woman lying on her back close to the flight of steps leading into the yard. Her throat was cut in a fearful manner. The woman's body had been completely ripped open and the heart and other organs laying about the place, and portions of the entrails round the victim's neck. An excited crowd gathered in front of Mrs. Richardson's house and also round the mortuary in old Montague Street, whither the body was quickly conveyed. As the body lies in the rough coffin in which it has been placed in the mortuary the same coffin in which the unfortunate Mrs. Nicholl was first placed it presents a fearful sight. The body is that of a woman about 45 years of age. The height is exactly five feet. The complexion is fair, with wavy brown hair; the eyes are blue, and two lower teeth have been knocked out. The nose is rather large and prominent.

and knife were simply work associated items. He was, without doubt, an unsavoury character and a general nuisance, but totally innocent of murder, in the wrong place at the wrong time. The newshounds had smelled a quarry guaranteed to boost circulation, rumours spread far and wide, and Leather Apron soon achieved international fame, his persona becoming increasingly distorted as the newsworthy scoop travelled across the Atlantic.

The dispatches this morning give a description in detail of the midnight assassin alleged to have perpetrated the murder of Mary Ann Nichols. The victim was literally cut to pieces with a knife in the hands of a mysterious being, whose footsteps could not be heard, whilst those of the woman resounded in the shadows as she fled from her murderer. The crime has shocked the whole of England, and is generally charged to a short, thickset, half-crazy creature, with fiendish black eyes, and known as 'Leather Apron.' He frequented the dark alleys, and like a veritable imp, haunted the gloom of the passageways of Whitechapel, and lived by robbing the female Arabs who roamed the streets after nightfall. Of powerful muscle, carrying a knife which he brandished over his victims, the London murder fiend was too terrible an assailant for the victim that cowered beneath the glitter of cold steel. He is charged with two other murders of women besides Mary Ann Nichols. Austin Statesman, Texas. 5 September 1888.

In the event, John Pizer was soon released from internment, the press announced his innocence, and at least one newspaper paid compensation. The hapless Sergeant Thicke was apparently not available for comment. The possible involvement of a leather apron, however, would doubtless have been the main topic of conversation through the haze of cigar smoke in Masonic Lodges throughout the land, as eyebrows were raised, monocles dropped into the soup, and brandy consumption doubled at the realisation that the Whitechapel Murderer may have been one of their own. Brother Sir Charles Warren, however, was still blissfully unaware that he was about to be drawn personally into the nightmare by a fellow Freemason, hateful of harlotry, and unforgiving of rejection.

ANNIE CHAPMAN

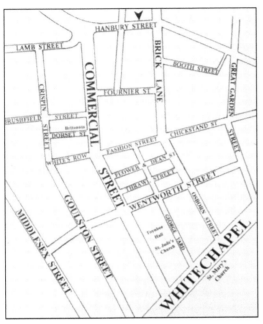

Early in the morning of the 8th September, Annie Chapman, a prostitute since the death of her husband in 1886, was short of money to purchase a bed in Crossinghams Lodging House in Dorset Street. At 1.35 am, sporting a black eye from a pub fight two days earlier, 'Dark Annie', as she was known locally, set off in the direction of Spitalfield Market, telling the doss-house keeper to reserve her bed, as she would soon be back. Four hours later, Annie Chapman lay dead in the back yard of No. 29 Hanbury Street, off Commercial Street, north of Toynbee Hall and St. Jude's Church.

The wounds inflicted were exactly similar to those which caused the death of the woman Nichols eight days before. Nichols, it will be remembered, was found with her throat cut, and frightfully mutilated, upon the pavement of Buck's Row. Rather more than three weeks previously, Martha Tabram was picked up dead on the stairs of George Yard Buildings, Whitechapel, with 39 stab wounds on her body. The police believe that the murder has been committed by the same person who perpetrated the three previous ones in the district, and that only one person is concerned in it. This person, whoever he may be, is doubtless labouring under some terrible form of insanity, as each of the crimes has been of the most fiendish character, and it is feared that, unless he can speedily be captured, more outrages of a similar class will be committed. The most salient point is the maniacal frenzy with which the victims were slaughtered, and, unless we accept, as a possible alternative, the theory that the assassin was activated by revenge for some real or supposed injury suffered by him at the hands of unfortunate women, we are thrown back on the belief that these murders were really committed by a madman. The Times. 10 September 1888.

The inquest was opened at two o'clock that afternoon, with Dr. George Bagster Phillips, Surgeon to the Metropolitan Police, providing a limited description of the corpse, which by then had been identified by her friend Amelia Farmer.

Dr. Phillips: The legs were drawn up, the feet resting on the ground and the knees turned outwards. The face was swollen and turned on the right side, and the tongue protruded between the front teeth. The small intestines and other portions were lying on the ground above the right shoulder, but attached. The throat was dis-severed deeply, the incision of the skin was jagged and right round the neck.

Dr. Bagster Phillips was undoubtedly aware that not only was this the work of a seriously deranged individual, but h e was the only person in the courtroom aware of the full extent of the mutilations. As Surgeon to the Metropolitan Police, Dr. Phillips had evidently discussed the matter in great depth with senior officials in the Home Office, and all indications are that he was under instruction from powerful figures in the Establishment to suppress the evidence.

Coroner: The object of the inquest is not only to ascertain the cause of death, but the means by which it occurred. Mutilation that took afterwards may suggest the character of the man that

74

The Inquest of Annie Chapman.

did it.   Possibly you can give the conclusions to which you have come.

Dr. Phillips: I think if it is possible to escape the details it would be advisable. The cause of death is visible from that described.

Coroner: You have kept a record of them?

Dr. Phillips: I have.

Coroner: We will postpone that for the present. You can give your own opinion as to how death was caused.

Dr. Phillips proceeded to explain that the thickening of the tongue indicated partial strangulation prior to cutting of the throat, and responded to questions unrelated to the major wounds.   After other witnesses had been heard, the inquest was adjourned, and re-opened on the 20th September, when Dr. Phillips was once again called as a witness.

Coroner: Whatever may be your opinion and objections, it appears to me necessary that all the evidence that you ascertain from the post-mortem examination should be on the Court for various reasons which I need not enumerate.

Dr. Phillips: I will do my best.   I still think it is a very great pity to make the evidence public.   When I come to speak on the wounds on the lower part of the body, I must again repeat my opinion that it is highly injudicious to make the results of my examination public.   These details are fit only for yourself, sir, and the jury, but to make them public would be disgusting.   In giving these details to the public, I believe you are thwarting the ends of justice.

Coroner: We are bound to take all the evidence in the case, and whether it be made public or not is a matter for the responsibility of the press.

Jury Foreman: We are of the opinion that the evidence the doctor on his last occasion wished to keep back should be heard.

Coroner: I have carefully considered the matter, and have never before heard of any evidence requested being kept back.

Dr. Phillips: I have not kept it.   I have only suggested whether it should be given or not.

Coroner: We have delayed taking this evidence as long as possible, because you said the interests of justice might be served by keeping it back, but it is now a fortnight since this occurred, and I do not see why it should be kept back from the jury any longer.

Dr. Phillips: I am of the opinion that what I am about to describe took place after death, so that it could not affect the cause of death, which you are inquiring into.

Coroner: That is only your opinion, and might be repudiated by the medical opinion.

Dr. Phillips: Very well, I will give you the results of the post-mortem examination.   The abdomen had been laid entirely open; the intestines, severed from their mesenteric attachments, had been lifted out of the body and been placed on the shoulder of the corpse;   whilst from the pelvic section, the uterus and its appendages, with the upper part of the vagina and the posterior two thirds of the bladder, had been entirely removed. No trace of these parts could be found, and the incisions were clearly cut, avoiding the rectum, and dividing the vagina low enough to avoid injury to the cervix uteri.

Evidence was next heard from Elizabeth Long, the last person to see Annie Chapman alive.

On Saturday, September 8th, about half past five in the morning, I was passing down Hanbury Street from home on my way to Spitalfield Market. I knew the time because I heard the brewer's clock strike half-past five, just before I got to the street. I passed 29 Hanbury Street. On the right-hand side, the same side as the house, I saw a man and a woman standing on the pavement talking. The man's head was turned towards Brick Lane, and the woman's was towards the market. They were standing only a few yards nearer Brick Lane from Hanbury Street. I saw the woman's face. I have seen the deceased in the mortuary. I did not see the man's face, but I noticed that he was dark. He was wearing a low-crowned felt hat. I think he had on a dark coat, though I am not certain. By the look of him he seemed to be a man over forty years of age. He appeared to be a little taller than the deceased. He looked like a foreigner. I should say he looked like what I should call shabby genteel. I overheard him say to her 'Will you', and she replied 'Yes'. That's all I heard as I passed. I left them standing there, and I did not look back.
Coroner: Was it not an unusual thing to see a man and woman talking?
Liz Long: Oh no. I see lots of them standing there in morning.
Coroner: At that hour of the day?
Liz Long: Yes, that is why I did not take much notice of them.

The next witness at the inquest was Albert Cadosch, living at No. 27 Hanbury Street, next door to where Annie Chapmans body was found in the back yard. He testified that at 5.15 am he went to the outside lavatory, and whilst in the yard, heard a voice from the other side of the fence say 'No'. A few minutes later he paid another visit, and heard something bumping into the fence, but instead of investigating, Albert went back to the lavatory, and in doing so forfeited national fame as the man who could have apprehended the Whitechapel Murderer.

No.29 Hanbury Street and the adjoining terraced properties were all lodging houses, in which it was common practice to leave the front doors on the latch, allowing lodgers to come and go at all hours. The inside hallway of the houses led straight through to the back door, giving access to the rear yard, and it was generally accepted that prostitutes made use of this arrangement to ply their trades, with little notice taken by the residents. An earlier client, seen with a prostitute at around 2.00 am in the rear yard of No.29 was the main suspect for a while, but nothing ever came of it, other than rumours that it was 'Leather Apron' again. Just before 6.00 am that morning, one of the lodgers, John Davies, discovered the body of Annie Chapman, lying on her back in the rear yard in a pool of blood. On later examination, an abrasion was noted over the ring finger, with distinct markings of a ring or rings having been removed. Edward Stanley, a longstanding friend of Annie Chapman, had seen those rings previously.

Coroner: Was she wearing rings when you saw her?
Stanley: Yes. I believe two.
Coroner: What sort of rings were they, what was the metal?
Stanley: Brass, I should think by the look of them.

The rings had no monetary value, and must have been removed for a reason, a sentiment shared by Coroner Baxter, as he addressed the same question to another witness, William Stevens, who also confirmed that the deceased wore rings, a matter of specific interest to Brother Wynne Baxter, Past Master of Burlington Lodge No.96, already intrigued by the possible Masonic significance of the mutilations.

On Friday night the murdered woman had worn three rings, which were not genuine, but were imitations. It has definitely been ascertained that the woman did wear two rings at the time of her death. They were of brass. One was a wedding ring, and the other a keeper of fancy pattern. Both are missing, and the police are still searching for them. The Star. 10 September 1888.

There were two things missing. Her rings had been wrenched from her fingers, and have not since been found, and the uterus had been taken from the abdomen. The brute who had committed the offence did not even take the trouble to conceal his ghastly work, but left the body exposed to the view of the first comers.
.   The Times. 20 September 1888.

Near the body were found a piece of muslin material, two combs, and a torn envelope on which was the letter 'M', the first of a series of obtuse clues which were to become an inherent factor in an ongoing game being played out in human lives.

A portion of an envelope was found lying where the head had been, and a piece of paper containing two pills. On the back of the envelope was the seal of the Sussex Regiment. The other portion of the writing was torn away. On the other side of the envelope was the letter 'M' in a man's handwriting.
.   The Times. 14 September 1888.

This was the first indication of a mischievous side to the Whitechapel murderer. To Michael Maybrick, the 'M' referred to his own Middlesex Regiment, as opposed to the Sussex Regiment. A typical Maybrick red herring. Also 'M' for Maybrick. Hilarious, and only he understood.

Annie Chapman was 47 years old, stoutly built, with brown hair, and was five feet in height. Given Liz Long's evidence that the man was 'slightly taller', the police should have been seeking a five feet two inch Toulouse Lautrec lookalike, who would very likely have come off worse in a tussle with pub brawler Annie Chapman. As a witness, Liz Long's integrity is not in doubt, but it was revealed that three days had passed before she presented her recollections of the couple to the police, following a press appeal for witnesses. By her own admission, she had taken no notice of the pair, as the presence of couples in Hanbury Street at that time of morning was seemingly commonplace. There was no indication that they were acting suspiciously, nor were they any more memorable than any other couple seen over the previous few days. Liz Long's memory must have been vague at best.

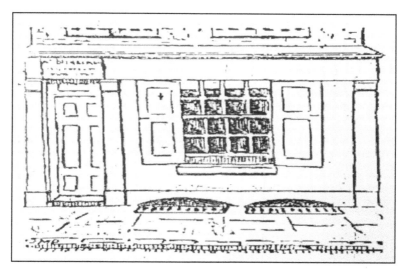

29 Hanbury Street. The Star. 8 September 1888.

Given that the man was aware of Liz's imminent approach, then moving Annie onto the step of the recessed doorway of No.29 would have been the logical course of action, which would have considerably narrowed down the couples difference in height. Engaged in conversation with a smaller woman, and anxious to conceal his height, a tall man would have bent his knees inside the long overcoat, adding further to the illusion. Liz did not see the man's face clearly, but by a miracle of perception, concluded that he was dark and looked foreign. Could there have been just a hint of beard? Dark and foreign would suffice, given the three day lapse in time. In Jewish Whitechapel in 1888, however, such a description covered a large portion of the populace, and was of no assistance whatsoever. Michael Maybrick's false black beard had served him well.

The earlier inquest on Mary Ann Nichols, deferred until 2nd September, ended with Coroner Wynn Baxter's poignant observation of the similarities between the murder of Emma Smith, Martha Tabram, Mary Ann Nichols and Annie Chapman.

We cannot altogether leave unnoticed the fact that the death you have been investigating is one of four presenting many points of similarity, all of which have taken place within the space of about five months, and all within a very short distance of the place where we are sitting. All four victims were women of middle age, all were married, and had lived apart from their husbands because of intemperate habits, and were at the time of their death leading an irregular life, and eking out a miserable and precarious existence in common lodging houses. In each case there were abdominal as well as other injuries. In each case the injuries were inflicted after midnight, and in places of public resort, where it would appear impossible but that immediate detection should follow the crime. The audacity and daring is equal to its maniacal fanaticism and abhorrent wickedness.
.   Coroner Wynne Baxter

Horrific as these events were, the shocked residents of Whitechapel seemed to have recovered from their trauma in no time at all.

For several hours, the occupants of the adjoining house in Hanbury Street have been charging an admission fee of one penny for people to view the spot where the body was found, though all that can be seen are a couple of packing cases, from beneath which is the stain of blood track. Several hundreds of people have availed themselves of this opportunity. .

.   The Star. 8 September 1888.

Will you kindly allow a little space in your paper to call the attention of your readers to what can only be considered a public nuisance and disgrace. I refer to the several low penny shows at the corner of Thomas Street and Whitechapel Road, facing the London Hospital. These sinks of iniquity are at the present time doing a roaring trade, by exhibiting horrible pictures representing the poor victims who have been so brutally murdered of late. Great crowds stand gazing at these bloodstained pictures. Meanwhile the pickpockets are making the best use of their opportunity. It is truly painful to hear the jostling and trifling talk about these things so awful.

The Echo, London. 11 September 1888.

Sir, Being a tradesman of Whitechapel, I wish to have a few words on your article of the 11th, about the disgraceful scenes that have been going on lately in the neighbourhood. It is not safe for a respectable person to walk the streets whilst the nuisances are going on. Another great nuisance which I think the police ought to put a stop to the Italian organs which infest our streets day and night. They cause large crowds of boys and girls, men and women, to assemble for the purpose of dancing. I was passing through a street only last Friday evening, when I noticed a drunken woman, with a baby that appeared to be five months old, running round and trying to dance to one of those organs, the poor child half naked and crying, while drunken men and women were enjoying the fun. I am sure the police will do their best to quell these disturbances. Yours

The Echo. 12 September 1888.

Having earlier described G.F. Watts's artistic contributions to St. Jude's Church, the reporter from the Globe continued his tour of Whitechapel, recounting the realities of street life.

And so thinking, I passed out into the street, for previous to having a talk with Mr. Barnett, I desired to refresh my remembrance of the squalid scenes of the recent murders. Three minutes walk takes one from the quiet light of the church, with its solemn thoughts and memories, into the midst of Wentworth Street, and what a change it is. There you see the most sordid life of London in everyday aspect. To say that the street is crowded is but to give the very faintest idea of what it is like. A pedestrian can hardly screw his way through among stalls bearing wedges of cake, or cairns of loaves, apparently all crust, or great heaps of socks which appear to be all single, or jockey's caps, or trousers, or underclothing. It is like Brick Lane, save there are fewer sellers of cheap jewellery, beautiful gold rings, 'See the 'all mark inside,' shouts the vendor, 'and the perfect finish, only one penny each'. And the women crowd round and buy the rubbish, three or four at a time, to be worn on their fingers, and often torn off after death, as was the case with Mrs. Chapman. The Globe. 20 September 1888.

There were widely divergent views on the efficiency of the newly formed Vigilance Committees, including this satirical commentary in the Pall Mall Gazette.

The Whitechapel murder is no doubt very foul, loathsome and horrible. But when all is said and done, that is no reason why people should go stark staring mad over it. It is difficult to regard one suggestion made on Saturday as the product of anything but sheer lunacy. The people of East London, we are told, must form themselves at once into Vigilance Committees, which should devote themselves to volunteer work at night. They should be cautioned to work in couples. Whistles and a signalling system should be provided, and the means of summoning a rescue force should be at hand. The suggestion that every unfortunate in London should be shadowed by a couple of respectable householders with reserves in the rear, ready to rush up on hearing a whistle, is the one gleam of irresistible comic in the whole of this gruesome tragedy. We incline on the whole to the belief that the murderer is a victim of erotic mania, which often takes the awful shape of an uncontrollable taste for blood. The Marquis de Sade was an amiable looking gentleman, and so, possibly enough, may be the Whitechapel murderer.

The Pall Mall Gazette. 10 September 1888.

Vigilance Association Members. Illustrated London News. 13 October 1888.

One amiable looking gentleman was particularly well served by such legitimised nightly forays with the St. Jude's Vigilance Association.

The first of the four Whitechapel murders having been committed immediately in the rear of Toynbee Hall, a Vigilance Committee was set on foot to second the efforts of the police in the discovery and prevention of crime. Since the latest tragedy, the exertions of the Committee have been re-doubled. Much voluntary help has been tended, one of the progenitors being a military officer, residing in Western London.

Lloyds Weekly Newspaper.
16 September 1888.

Serving military officers would have been precluded from engaging in such activities, but not so civilians from volunteer reserve units. One such pillar of society, resplendent in full military attire, was clearly intent on impressing the Lloyds reporter with his status as founder member of St Jude's Vigilance Association, the most ingenious and enduring false alibi in British criminal history. At the same time, the dashing hero was modestly courting anonymity, subtly placing on record his place of residence in Regent's Park, West London, well away from the murderer's assumed lair in London's East End.

Rewards were offered by sectors of the press and by private individuals, but none was forthcoming from the Home Office, which was resolutely against the proposal. On the 15th September, the newly formed Whitechapel Vigilance Committee, a separate organisation constituted one month after that of St. Jude's, under the leadership of Mr. George Lusk, wrote directly to the Home Secretary, Henry Matthews, requesting that he reconsider his views on the matter. On the 17th September, the Home Office dutifully replied,

Whitechapel. 17 September 1888.

Sir, I am directed by the Secretary of State to acknowledge receipt of your letter of the 16th inst. With reference to the question of

the offer of a reward for the recovery of the discovery of the perpetrators of the recent murders in Whitechapel, I am to inform you that, had the Secretary of State considered it proper for the offer of a reward, he would have offered one on behalf of the Government, but the practice of offering rewards for the discovery of criminals was discontinued some years ago, because experience showed that such offers of reward tended to produce more harm than good. The Secretary of State is satisfied that there is nothing in the circumstances of the present case to justify a departure from this rule.

The Morning Post.
20 September 1888.

Dr. Bagster Phillips had fought fiercely and valiantly to suppress the nature of Annie Chapman's mutilations, but Coroner Wynne Baxter had won the day. Having failed on that front, the full weight of the Home Office was brought to bear on the press, to ensure the details went no further than the courtroom. Not one newspaper report on the inquest related the nature of the sexual mutilations, with press articles limited to phrases such as the 'witness then detailed the terrible wounds which had been inflicted on the woman.' Word was soon out, however, that the uterus had been removed, but, instead of pursuing the seemingly obvious conclusion that the killer had taken it for his own gratification, press articles either pursued the theory that the kidney had been stolen for medical purposes, or avoided the topic altogether.

Strings were clearly being pulled behind the scenes to stifle the facts, but nothing could contend with street gossip, or contain the wave of fear that the victims' internal organs had been taken for nefarious reasons by a sex maniac, and the press soon warmed up to public opinion, proclaiming the obvious conclusion that a serial killer was at large, and would kill again.

FUNNY LITTLE GAMES

By early September, four lives had been claimed, and a pattern was emerging. Similar characteristics are often displayed in a serial killer's choice of victims, but on occasions an underlying and less obvious link becomes apparent, of particular significance to the perpetrator. All the victims had been prostitutes of similar age, height, hair colour, and build, personifying the Liverpool prostitute responsible for so much physical and emotional trauma, resulting in impotence, possible sexual disfiguration, and the onset of a form of neurosyphilis, with all the consequences. The first two, Emma Smith and Martha Tabram, known locally as Emma, and tagged as such in the morgue, very likely had the same name as the Liverpool whore, the very mention of whom triggered the psychotic need for revenge.

Prior to his joining the Middlesex Rifles and discovering Toynbee Hall, Michael Maybrick had learned to live with his obsessive hatred of Emma, who had robbed him of his masculinity, and deprived him of enjoying the affections of so many attractive and readily available women. Hitherto, he had deliberately avoided areas notorious for prostitution, but now he was in the hotbed of Whitechapel, approached by whores practically every time on leaving Toynbee Hall, or St. Jude's Church, more than one of whom closely resembled that woman from Liverpool, resulting in sleepless nights, nightmares, and a burning realisation that revenge was possible at last. Michael Maybrick became a pathologically unstable man on a mission, obsessively brooding on the name of Emma, repeating it, loathing it, dissecting it, just like the bodies in the Museum of Anatomy, and just as he would dissect the whore once he laid hands on her.

In the same way as a musical note is divisible into two minims, in Maybrick's musically honed mind Emma was divisible into 'Emm' and 'A' resulting in the letters 'MA', also the first letters of his own surname, seemingly irrational to a normal person, but in the disturbed mind of this classical composer, a perfect configuration. Michael Maybrick had been well grounded from childhood in the refinement of musical notes, a devotee of pen to paper, but no longer of a normal mindset, distorted as it was in adolescence by the physiological effects of his traumatic encounter with Emma.

Emma, (Em Ma) 'MA', were a logical progression, giving rise to an amusing concept, which would be orchestrated into a funny little game. Why not collect more letters? A whore with those letters in her name was in for trouble.

This fantasy soon developed into a fixation, and 'MA' would become the trigger for violent outbursts against prostitutes, first manifested on Margaret Hames, assaulted in December 1887, shortly after Michael Maybrick's involvement with the military band at Toynbee Hall. Four months later, Emma Smith, possessing the actual name, as well as the 'MA' factor, would find herself the subject of very special treatment, at a carefully planned meeting place.

After a night of Spring Bank Holiday revelry at Toynbee Hall with the band of the 20th Middlesex Rifles, Michael Maybrick made his way from the rear yard exit into Wentworth Street, and walked to his destination. Emma Smith, worse for wear after an earlier assault and robbery, made the turning into Brick Lane, just as arranged earlier. The location and the name of the chosen victim were deeply satisfying. Brick Lane and Emma would have meant absolutely nothing to the average person, but to

Michael Maybrick there was a glaringly obvious significance. Emma and Brick Lane were destined to be together.

EM(MA – BRICK) LANE

There was no evidence of a crime scene in Brick Lane, so why the specific reference to No. 10, Brick Lane in Inspector Edmund Reid's report? This was a pre-arranged meeting place which must have been imprinted in the victim's memory, and related to her friend Mary Russell, who included the detail in her witness statement.

If Michael Maybrick had intended to kill Emma Smith, he could easily have done so there and then, but the intention was to wreak revenge, to cause serious sexual injury, pain, and humiliation, just as he had experienced. Emma had been left semi-conscious, but once her death was announced the following day, the dreadful consequence struck home, with the prospect of judicial execution, preceded by disgrace, dishonour, and rejection by his peers and admirers. This was the point of no return, and entirely the whore's fault. More would now pay the price at the whim of Michael Maybrick, and in a manner of his own choosing.

Five months after Spring Bank Holiday, the arrival of August Bank Holiday weekend saw the band of the 20th Middlesex Rifles once again at Toynbee Hall, featuring the celebrated baritone Michael Maybrick, who had already selected his next victim, also named 'Emma', living in nearby George Street, and working the area around Wentworth Street. The celebrations at Toynbee Hall proved a roaring success, so very reminiscent of the Spring Bank Holiday, and Michael Maybrick, waiting at the rear exit from Toynbee Hall in Wentworth Street, was about to re-live the satisfaction of wreaking revenge on the Liverpool whore. Later that morning, Emma's body was found in George Yard

Building, just to the rear of Toynbee Hall, twenty seconds walk away.

Days later, the body was identified, not as Emma, but as Martha Tabram, which at first came as a surprise to her murderer, soon placated by the unforeseen inclusion of the 'MA' factor in Martha's name, attributed, of course, to divine providence. Whilst musing on the name, it soon became apparent to the now dedicated cryptologist that 'Martha Tabram' included seven of the letters in 'Michael Maybrick', and the concept of a Funny Little Game was about to evolve.

The ensuing game plan has to be viewed through the disturbed mind of an extremely intelligent man, subliminally motivated by unconventional thought patterns, deriving satisfaction from plucking letters from the names of potential victims, and dissecting their identities to create his own name, the name of their executioner, the ultimate manifestation of total control. Crazy, but not so in the rationale of Michael Maybrick, psychopath, but also child prodigy, fond of wordplay, with a predilection for anagrams, rhymes and cryptograms, long before the introduction of the crossword puzzle.

Crucial to such intentions, however, would be a search for suitable candidates, seemingly impossible without incurring the risk of exposure to suspicion. Then, two or three days later, Michael Maybrick's spiritual mentor inspired the concept of forming the St. Jude's Vigilance Association, given added credibility by the military experience of one or two members of the Artist's Rifles, the ideal means of infiltration into the populace of Whitechapel, whilst arousing no suspicion whatsoever. This outrageous Funny Little Game was as challenging as any musical composition, but instead of melodies, was to be played out in human lives.

On the 23rd September 1888, there appeared in the pages of Punch Magazine a cartoon lampooning the ability of the police to apprehend the Whitechapel Murderer. Beneath was a caption 'Turn round three times, and catch whom you may.' The author of the 'Maybrick Diary' clearly found this a great source of amusement, making great play of the word May.

BLIND-MAN'S BUFF.

(As played by the Police)

"TURN ROUND THREE TIMES,
AND CATCH WHOM YOU MAY."

I could not stop laughing when I read Punch. There for all to see was the first three letters of my surname. I cannot stop laughing, it amuses me, so shall I write them a clue? 'With a ring on my finger and a knife in my hand, this May spreads Mayhem throughout this fair land.' Shirley Harrison. Diary of Jack the Ripper.

Was Michael Maybrick known to some of his friends and colleagues as 'May'? In spoken form, the letters MA phonetically include the word May, and what fun to claim the identity of a victim by covertly extracting from their names the name of the inescapable nemesis of their impending downfall. Compounded with the traumatic association of the same letters with the name Emma, the letters MA were a catalyst for trouble.

By now a notebook had been diligently compiled, containing the names of a small number of unfortunates with the qualifying letters 'MA' within their names, encountered in the course of night patrols under the subterfuge of the St. Jude's Vigilance Association. The list was then further refined to those with the appropriate physical characteristics, and after endless hours of scheming, Mary Ann Nichols was found to fulfil the necessary requirements

EM<u>MA</u> SMITH
<u>MA</u>RTHA TABRAM
<u>MA</u>RY ANN NICHOLS

Next, consider those who had narrowly escaped death at his hands, having been attacked spontaneously when encountered on the nights in question.

<u>MA</u>RGARET HAMES
<u>MA</u>LVINA HAYNES
<u>MA</u>RGARET MILLOUS

The murder and mutilation of Martha Tabram had instigated the first phase of the Funny Little Game, which had started with the 'MA' factor. Inspiration had been ignited within the electrically charged brain of a psychopath, endowed with the ingenuity and intelligence of a classical composer, and the guile and ruthlessness of a wolf. Kill one, and the rest are just numbers ….. or indeed letters. Starting with Martha Tabram, letters forming the name of Michael Maybrick would be plucked from the names of deliberately selected victims. Within the seriously demented mind of the killer, this was a way of asserting ultimate control over his victims, neutralising their very existence by depriving them of their very identities, out of which he would create his own name.

MARTHA TABRAM   **M**HA**   MA*BR*****
MARY ANN NICHOLS   **MICHA*L MAYBR*****

All that was required to complete his name were four missing letters 'EICK'. One week later, Annie Chapman's life was snuffed out, obligingly providing the letters 'EIC' of the missing four letters, as well as the obligatory 'MA', required for inclusion on the shortlist.

MARTHA TABRAM   **M**HA** MA*BR*****
MARY ANN NICHOLS **MICHA*L MAYBR*****
ANNIE CHAPMAN   **MICHAEL MAYBRIC***

It was now just a matter of time before the fulfilment of Michael Maybrick's malevolent scheme, the satisfaction of drawing his own name from the souls of his struggling, dying victims, the ultimate expression of dominance, control and revenge, a deadly but immensely satisfying little game. By the date of the Punch Cartoon, on the 23rd September 1888, all that was required to complete the game was a victim whose name contained the letter 'K', and, of course, the qualifying letters 'MA'. The vigilante's notebook held the answer.

MARY ANN KELLY

The name of the next murder victim was in the notebook, the site had already been planned, and it was ever so funny. How better to tantalise Brother Charles Warren than to murder a whore 'on the square', one of the traditional phrases used by Freemasons to identify one another.   Even better, select the next site frustratingly outside the jurisdiction of the Metropolitan Police, where Brother Warren could only watch as the rival City Police handled proceedings. Mitre Square it would be. Hilarious.

Meticulous planning was the determining factor between success and the hangman's noose, and a second base was advisable, well away from St. Jude's.   With no wife or immediate family in London, and travelling the country's theatres on a regular basis, Michael Maybrick was totally unaccountable, and a casual room rental, paid in advance and unused for most of the time, would prove ideal, especially if the need were to arise for retreat in a different direction. Suppose that Michael Maybrick, posing as a businessman from the City, made enquiries in the area between the Royal Mint and the Tower of London, relatively close to Whitechapel, but almost devoid of people late at night, deliberately chosen as not being subject to routine police checks, unlike residential lodgings in Whitechapel, which had been heavily targeted latterly.   A police interview, revealed later, indicates a base in King Street, a quiet road predominantly occupied by immigrant tailors, empty at night, and with a link of alleyways, lanes and hidden courtyards leading through to Aldgate and Mitre Square. Perfect.

Since early Victorian times, the hop-fields of Kent had traditionally attracted a seasonal migration in September of poor

London families and couples, leaving behind the slums and doss-houses of Whitechapel for a working holiday in the countryside, enjoying healthy food and accommodation in rows of hopping huts. John and Mary Kelly had been working in the hop-fields for three weeks, and at the close of season towards the end of September, they trudged 35 miles from the open countryside back to the grime of Whitechapel, soon learning that a reward of £100 had been offered by Samuel Montagu, MP for Whitechapel, for

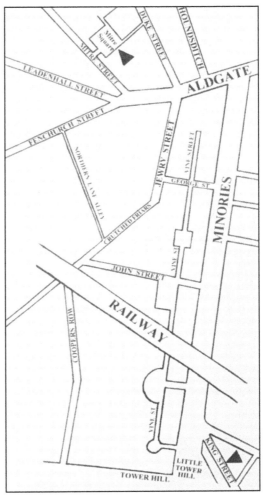

information leading to the capture of the Whitechapel Murderer.

Mary may well have been in Michael Maybrick's sights in the course of his vigilante wanderings before leaving for the Kent hopfields, and there are indications that on her return she soon became aware of the enticement which had been offered to secure the arrest of the killer.

A reporter gleaned some curious information from the Casual Wards Superintendent of Mile End regarding the Mitre Square victim, formerly well known in the casual wards there, but who had disappeared for a considerable time until the Friday preceding her murder. Asking the woman where she had been in the interval, the superintendent was met with the reply she had been in the country, hopping, 'But' added the woman, 'I have come back to earn the reward for the apprehension of the Whitechapel Murderer. I think I know him.' 'Mind he doesn't murder you too,' replied the superintendent jocularly. 'Oh, no fear of that,' was the reply as she left. .

East London Observer. 13 October 1888.

Had contact already been made? *'I have come back to earn the reward'*, would certainly indicate so. In the event, Mary soon returned to her old habits, and at 8.30 pm on Saturday, 29th September, was arrested in Aldgate High Street for being drunk and incapable, and was taken to Bishopsgate Police Station to sober up. Newspapers cost a halfpenny, but street talk cost nothing, and news travelled fast, with word of Mary's detention having been passed around from the moment she was arrested, as testified at the later inquest by her partner, John Kelly.

I last saw her on Saturday afternoon, in Houndsditch. I heard afterwards that she had been locked up on Saturday night. A woman who works in the lane told me this, and said she had been taken to the station. John Kelly.

Assuming Mary had been a person of interest before the hop-picking break, primed with the prospect of a reward, it would not have been too difficult for Michael Maybrick to encounter her that afternoon, prior to her arrest, and arrange a later meeting in Mitre Square. Mary had certainly obtained her ale money from someone earlier in the day, possibly courtesy of a trusted member of the local Vigilance Association, possessor of valuable information on the identity of the Whitechapel Murderer. Given the prospect of £100 reward once in possession of information promised later that night, a few beers were definitely called for. Unfortunately, Mary just didn't know when to stop. Once Maybrick heard of Mary's arrest, he had to work fast. It seems 1.00 am was the generally accepted cut-off time in Whitechapel for doss house lodgers to pay for their beds, and it was the unwritten rule in police stations to adopt that hour as the time to clear out drunks from the cells, or the prospect of a bed in the police station overnight, free of charge, would have filled every available police cell in East London every night of the week.

Mary was released from Bishopsgate Police Station at 1.00 am, giving her details as Mary Ann Kelly, 6 Fashion Street. Mary had very recently pawned a pair of boots, giving her details as Jane Kelly, 6 Dorset Street, proving that she was not averse to the occasional change of name and address when it suited, particularly when it came to different names on a police record sheet. Michael Maybrick knew her as Mary Ann Kelly.

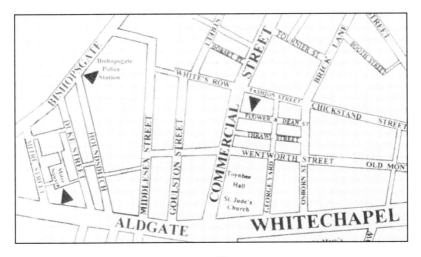

The duty sergeant at Bishopsgate Police Station advised as follows,

I remember the deceased being brought to the Bishopsgate Station at a quarter to nine on the night of Saturday September 29ᵗʰ. She was very drunk, brought in supported by two constables and placed in a cell, where she remained until one o'clock the next morning when she had got sober. I then discharged her. She gave her name as Mary Ann Kelly, No. 6 Fashion Street, Spitalfields. She pulled the door to within a foot of being closed, and I saw her turn to the left, towards Houndsditch.

So, on leaving the police station, instead of heading towards her lodgings in Flower and Dean Street, less than 100 yards from Toynbee Hall, the duty policeman advised that Mary headed left towards Houndsditch, in the direction of Aldgate and Mitre Square, an area rarely frequented by ladies of the night, a decision which would cost her dearly.

LONG LIZ

Mary Ann Kelly may have been foremost in Michael Maybrick's mind when he set off with evil intent that evening, but totally unpredictably it would be a prostitute named Liz Stride who would come back to haunt him. A Swedish national, Liz had been living in England for twenty two years at the time of the Whitechapel murders, by which time she was engaged in regular prostitution. Known as 'Long Liz' on the streets of Whitechapel, 45 year old Liz had light grey eyes, curly dark brown hair, and was definitely not long by Whitechapel standards, at five feet five inches in height, with the origins of her anomalous street name unknown. An educated guess may be made, however, if reference is made to the police doctor's notes at the later inquest, which state 'There is deformity in the lower fifth of the bones in the right leg, which are not straight, but which bow forward. There is a thickening bone over the left ankle.' This would undoubtedly have caused Liz Stride to walk with a limp, giving rise to 'Limpalong Liz', shortened in no time on the cruel streets of Whitechapel to 'Long Liz'.

The night's events had been planned with military precision. The vigilante had left St. Jude's Church via Wentworth Street, dressed in normal attire, just after 12.30 am on the morning of the 30th September on a deliberately walkabout route, into Commercial Road and right into Berner Street, where the plan was to turn into Fairclough Street, and then on to Mitre Square via the room in King Street, for a change of clothes. However, all did not go to plan. Whilst making his way down Berner Street, keeping a low profile, Maybrick witnessed a street brawl on the opposite side of the road, outside the International Working Mens' Educational

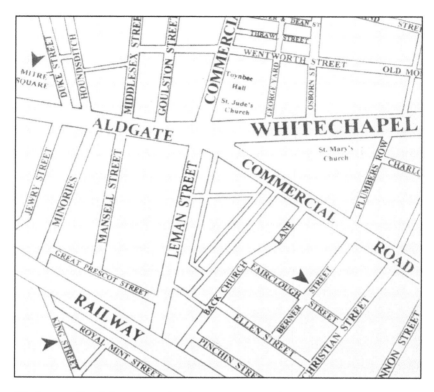

Club, a Jewish organisation engaged in radical socialist politics. The tussle involved a stranger and Liz, who Maybrick had acquainted on occasions in the course of his vigilante patrols. This was a serious dilemma. The clock was ticking towards the rendezvous with Mary Ann Kelly at 1.30 am, only 45 minutes away. Should he intervene, or leave poor Liz to suffer a severe beating or worse? Maybrick kept his head down, pretending to light the clay pipe he kept with him for subterfuge, and came to a decision. The first witness to the ensuing event was the man assaulting Liz on the street outside the club. The second was Michael Maybrick, and the third was Israel Schwartz, a Hungarian unable to speak English, who the following morning called into Leman Street Police Station accompanied by a friend, acting as interpreter. He was interviewed at length by Insp. Frederick Abberline, and the resultant interview was contained in a confidential report to the Home Office on the 19th October by Abberline's Superior, Chief Inspector Donald Swanson.

12.45 am, 30th September. Israel Schwartz, of 22 Helen Street, Backchurch Lane, stated that at that hour, on turning into Berner Street from Commercial Road, and having got so far as the gateway where the murder was committed, he saw a man stop to speak to a woman who was standing in the gateway. The man tried to pull the woman into the street, but he turned her round and threw her down on the footway, and the woman screamed three times, but not very loudly. On crossing to the opposite side of the street, he saw a second man lighting his pipe. The man who threw the woman down called out apparently to the man on the opposite side of the road 'Lipski', and then Schwartz walked away, but finding he was followed by the second man, he ran so far as the railway arch, but the man did not follow so far. Schwartz cannot say if the two men were together, or were known to each other. Upon being taken to the mortuary, Schwartz identified the body as that of the woman he had seen. He described the first man, who threw the woman down, aged about thirty, height 5 foot 5 inches, complexion fair, hair dark, small brown moustache, full faced, broad shouldered, dark jacket and trousers, black cap with peak. Second man aged 35, height 5 feet 11 inches, complexion fresh, hair light brown, moustache brown, dark overcoat, old black hard felt hat, wide brim, clay pipe in hand. Inspector Donald Swanson.

Later the same day, a slightly different version was provided by Israel Schwartz to a reporter from the Star newspaper.

Information which may be important was given to the Leman Street Police late yesterday afternoon by a Hungarian concerning the murder. The foreigner could not speak a word of English, but came to the police station with a friend, who acted as interpreter. He gave his name and address, but the police have not disclosed them.   A Star man, however, got wind of his call, and ran him to earth in Backchurch Lane.   The reporter's Hungarian was quite as imperfect as the foreigner's English, but an interpreter was at hand, and the man's story was re-told, just as he had given it to the police.   When he came homewards about a quarter before one, he first walked down Berner Street to see if his wife had moved.   As he turned the corner from Commercial Road, he noticed, some distance in front of him, a man walking as if partially intoxicated.   He walked on behind him, and presently he noticed a woman standing in the entrance to an alleyway, where afterwards the body was found.   The half tipsy man halted and spoke to her.   The Hungarian saw him put his hand on her shoulder and push her back into the passage, but feeling rather timid of getting mixed up in quarrels, he crossed to the other side of the street.   Before he had gone many yards, however, he heard the sounds of a quarrel, and turned back to see what was the matter.   Just as he stepped from the kerb, a second man came out of the doorway of the public house a few doors off, shouting out some sort of warning to the man who was with the woman, and rushed forward as if to attack the intruder.   The Hungarian states positively that he saw a knife in this man's hand, but he waited to see no more and fled.   He described the man with the woman as about 30 years of age, rather stoutly built, and wearing a brown moustache.   He was dressed respectably in dark clothes and felt hat.   The man who came at him with a knife he also describes, but not in detail.   He says he was taller than the other, but not so stout, and that his moustaches were red.   Both men seemed to belong to the same class of society.   The police have arrested one man answering the description the Hungarian furnishes.   The prisoner has not been charged, but is held for enquiries to be made.   The Star. 1 October 1888.

The press were not slow to realise that Inspector Abberline was not only reluctant to provide details, but, when he did, it was often with the usual blend of smoke and mirrors.   The assailant had evidently been detained in custody but not charged, leaving the tall man not only unaccounted for, but seemingly with minimal police effort directed towards finding him.

In investigating a crime, detectives proceed very quietly, often too quietly it might be thought, and, frequently through the agency of too credulous reporters, lead the really suspected person to believe that the scent lies in quite another quarter, while in reality his every movement is being closely watched. The Star. 3 October 1888.
.

In an internal memo one month later, Inspector Abberline, who had conducted the interviews with Israel Schwartz before passing his report to Chief Inspector Swanson, gives an indication that Schwartz's statements, whilst considered genuine, do contain uncertainties which allow for liberal interpretation.

With reference to the annexed copy extract from the Home Office letter, I questioned Israel Schwartz very closely at the time he made the statement as to whom the man addressed when he called 'Lipski', but he was unable to say. There was only one other person to be seen in the street, and that was a man on the opposite side of the road lighting a pipe. Schwartz being a foreigner, and unable to speak English, became alarmed and ran away. The man whom he saw lighting his pipe also ran in the same direction as himself, but whether this man was running after him or not he could not tell. He might have been alarmed the same as himself and ran away.

There is a great deal of difference between a clay pipe as in the police statement, and a knife, as in the newspaper article, and both the Hungarian and Yiddish words for each are totally dissimilar, with no possibility of mistranslation. Was the second man keeping his head down, on the pretext of pretending to light a pipe, whilst at the same time working out how to carry on down the road without being recognised? Perhaps also, whilst the press were obviously not privy to the police reports, Detectives

103

Swanson and Abberline had no wish either to disclose too much information to meddling Home Office Officials, and worded the report in less alarming tones than disclosed in the later Star report. One suspect was quite enough, no need to murky the waters. In the event, however, both the police report and the Star report do have some links in common, which merit consideration.

Take the 'Lipski' utterance. Could it have been the 'second man' shouting 'Lipski', and not the assailant? In the police report, Schwartz states the man who threw the woman down called out 'Lipski', apparently to the man on the opposite side of the road. Yet, in the Star report, Schwartz states 'a second man came out of the doorway of the public house a few doors off, shouting out some sort of warning to the man who was with the woman, and rushed forward as to attack the intruder.'

What was the origin of the phrase 'Lipski'? Israel Lipski was a Jewish immigrant, formerly living in the next road to Berner Street, and executed the previous year for battering and murdering his landlady, with the word 'Lipski' subsequently entering Whitechapel street parlance as a term of abuse, usually directed at Jewish immigrants. Did the mysterious 'second man' in Berner Street call out 'Lipski' at the assailant in the context of a woman beater? Was Michael Maybrick, in his role as gallant vigilante, calling out impulsively, without realising he had inadvertently instigated a confrontation with an angry, broad shouldered, albeit shorter man? Israel Schwartz, minding his own business and with eyes down, probably heard the word 'Lipski' at the same time as the assailant, and was uncertain from whom the word had emanated. It came from Michael Maybrick, warrior bold, adept at killing small defenceless women, but now faced, for the first time in his life, with the prospect of real physical conflict, and, even worse, police involvement.

As the assailant stared up at him in response to the vocal intervention, Lieutenant Maybrick of the 20th Middlesex (Artists) Rifle Volunteers would have experienced fear, instinctively reaching for the small sharp knife he always carried, flashing just enough steel to act as a threat, without inviting combat. Thankfully, this proved sufficient to send Schwartz and the assailant scurrying off into the distance, followed for effect by a few paces of feigned pursuit by the intrepid hero, extremely thankful not to have had his precious good looks marred by a black eye. The tail end of the incident was endorsed by William Wess, Secretary of the Working Men's Club, who described the flight, which was actually Israel Schwartz followed not far behind by the assailant.

In the course of conversation, says the journalist, the secretary mentioned the fact that the murderer had no doubt been disturbed in the work, as about a quarter to one o' clock on Sunday morning, he was seen, or at least a man whom the public prefer to regard as the murderer, being chased by another man along Fairclough Street. The man being pursued escaped, however, and the secretary of the Club cannot remember the name of the man who gave chase, but he is not a member of their body.

. The Echo. 1 October 1888.

Within this report are inconsistencies indicating that the tale was a hearsay re-hash of Israel Schwartz's story. Had Wess seen the event, he would have been around to witness the murder, and he was not. Wess conveniently could not 'remember' the name of the second man, inferring familiarity, and as Schwartz lived in the immediate locality, he was very probably known to Wess, or indeed Wess may have been acting as his interpreter, resolving to stay silent on the matter. The reality is that both men in the report, one of whom was Schwartz, were in flight from the tall interloper with the knife, rather than one chasing the other.

Whoever had been the first to take to his heels would have kept on running, without turning to see who was behind him. Bear in mind, Michael Maybrick was on edge, well adept in the use of a knife, with at least four murders to his tally already, and even in low streetlight, his eyes probably conveyed a very serious message, sufficient to send two men scurrying off into the night, in fear of their lives.

The whole episode involving the assault probably lasted only around twenty seconds, although doubtless it would have seemed much longer to all concerned. Liz Stride would have been back on her feet, searching in her pocket for a comforting cachou sweet, when she realised she was all alone in the dark with the man who had flashed the knife. At this stage, Michael Maybrick probably wanted no more than to simply move on to Mitre Square, and complete the final part of his Funny Little Game, but Liz Stride had recognised him. Now there were only the two of them, alone on Berner Street. According to Schwartz' testimony, Liz had screamed earlier, and she probably screamed again, only to be quickly silenced by a pair of strong hands around her throat. No option at this stage. This woman had seen Michael Maybrick flash a knife, en route to a murder by appointment in Mitre Square, which would make the headlines the next day. Liz Stride was dragged unceremoniously backwards into the yard behind the Working Men's Club, held in a rear chokehold, and quickly dispatched with a deep slash to the throat. Hiss of air, gurgle of blood, dead weight as the body crumpled lifeless to the ground.

Dr. Blackwell, the first medical man called, says 'At about ten minutes past one I was called to Berner Street by a policeman, where I found a woman who had been murdered. Her head had been almost severed from her body. I roughly examined her, and found no other injuries. In her hand she held a box of cachous, and I should say that as the woman held sweets in her left hand, that her head was dragged back by means of a silk handkerchief she wore around her neck. I might say it does not follow that the murderer would be bespattered with blood, for as he is sufficiently cunning in other things, he could contrive to avoid coming into contact with the blood by reaching well forward. There is a severe bruise on the cheek of the unfortunate woman, which may be explained by the theory that the throat was cut while she was standing, and the body allowed to fall heavily upon its side, bringing the cheek into contact with a stone that abuts the wall just at this point. The woman was about 30 years of age. Her hair is very dark with a tendency to curl, and her complexion is also dark. The features are sharp and somewhat pinched, as though she had endured considerable privations recently, an impression confirmed by the entire absence of the kind of ornaments commonly affected by a woman of her station. She wore a rusty black dress of a cheap kind, with a velveteen bodice, over which was a black worsted jacket. Her bonnet, which had fallen from her head when she was found in the yard, was of black crepe, and inside, apparently with the object of making the article fit close to the head, was folded a newspaper. In the pockets of the woman's dress were discovered two handkerchiefs, a brass thimble, and a skein of darning worsted. The Star. 1 October 1888.

Such were the worldly possessions of the penniless Elizabeth Stride, her pathetic existence terminated in cold blood by the rich and famous Michael Maybrick. Minutes later, local salesman Louis Diemschutz drove his horse and cart into Duffield's Yard, and discovered the body at the rear of the Working Men's Club. This was the last intended place to commit a murder, but time was of the essence, and this unexpected and unplanned taste of blood, without the satisfaction of dissection, had fired up even more the psychopath within. Off poste-haste to the changing room in King Street, en route to the date with Mary Ann Kelly in Mitre Square.

Philip Kranz, working in the print room at the front of the working men's club, stated that even if a woman had screamed in the street outside, he would have heard nothing, due to the singing upstairs, which was loud. A dance was in progress at the club, and the occupants were engaged in a sing-a-long at the time of the murder, which, as well as creating a noise, would account for the lack of people emerging into the street for that short period of time. Pure luck, or in Michael Maybrick's quasi-religious mindset, the protecting wings of his guardian angel.

The boldness and audacity of the Berner Street murder becomes more and more apparent, as the circumstances under which it was committed are sifted. Not only were the lights in the International Working Men's Club all ablaze, but the side door, within three yards of which the murder was perpetrated, was ajar. Added to this was the additional danger of intrusion by any passer-by. Yet within two yards of the main thoroughfare, the poor woman met with her violent and untimely end.

.   Daily News. 2 October 1888.

Half an hour prior to the murder, Matthew Packer, owner of the little fruit stall next to the Working Men's Club, claims to have seen Liz Stride in the company of a man buying grapes from his stall. Having identified Liz Stride in the morgue, Packer described the man as aged twenty five to thirty years old, about five feet seven inches in height, with long black coat buttoned up, and rather broad shoulders. Israel Schwartz's description of Long Liz's assailant, as given to the police, was about thirty years old, height five feet five inches, dark hair, small black moustache, full faced, broad shouldered, dark jacket and trousers, black cap with peak. In the Star report, Schwartz described the same man as about 30 years of age, rather stoutly built, wearing a black moustache, and dressed respectably in dark clothes and felt hat.

Given that both witnesses on that fateful night were recalling sightings which would have had no significance at the time, and were under poor Victorian gas lighting, or in Packer's case, an old oil lamp on his stall, their recollections do have a marked similarity. Was the man seen by Packer the same man as seen by Schwartz, walking 'partially intoxicated' towards Liz Stride, and continuing an on-going drunken argument? According to the Star report, that man was soon detained in police custody, although not charged with any offence. Neither he, Israel Schwartz, or Matthew Packer were called to appear at the Stride inquest, despite being leading witnesses in Liz Stride's murder, which must raise questions as to whether information was indeed being deliberately suppressed. Apart from Inspector Abberline's personal lines of investigation, which remain undisclosed, the combined resources of the Metropolitan and City police forces had evidently produced no clues worthy of pursuit.

It is but fair to say that the police have clutched eagerly at every straw that promised to help them out, but there is nothing left to work on. People have come forward by scores to furnish the description of a man they had seen with some woman near the scene, but no two descriptions are alike. If every man should be arrested who was known to have been seen in company with an abandoned woman in that locality on last Saturday night, the police stations would not hold them. There are many people in that district who volunteer information to the police on the principle of securing lenient treatment for their own offences, and there are others who turn in descriptions on the chance of coming near enough the mark to claim a portion of the reward if the man should be caught, just as one buys a ticket in the lottery. Even where such information is given in good faith, it can rarely be looked upon in the light of a clue. The Star. 2 October 1888.

In his memoirs written twenty years later, Sir Robert Anderson,

Assistant Commissioner of Metropolitan Police at the time of the Whitechapel murders, provided a revealing insight into the misguided ineptitude of those in charge of the investigation at the time, glibly playing down the fact that he was relaxing in Europe whilst most of the murders had been taking place.

One did not need to be a Sherlock Holmes to discover that the criminal was a sexual maniac of a violent type, that he was living in the immediate vicinity of the scenes of the murders, and that, if he was not living absolutely alone, his people knew of his guilt, and refused to give him up to justice. During my absence abroad, the police had made a house to house search for him, and the conclusion we came to was that he and his people were certain low-class Polish Jews, for it is a remarkable fact that people of that class in the East End will not give up one of their number to Gentile justice. Having regard to the interest attaching to this case, I am almost tempted to disclose the identity of the murderer, but no public benefit would result from such a course, and the traditions of my old department would suffer. I will merely add that the only person who ever had a good view of the murderer unhesitatingly identified the suspect the instant he was confronted with him, but he refused to give evidence against him. The Lighter Side of my Official Life. Sir Robert Anderson 1910.

A copy of the book was presented by Sir Robert Anderson to Chief Inspector Donald Swanson, who pencilled the following notes in the margin alongside the above passage,

After the suspect had been identified at the seaside home where he had been sent by us with difficulty, in order to subject him to identification, he knew he was identified. In a very short time, the suspect, with his hands tied behind his back, was sent to Stepney Workhouse and then to Colney Hatch, and died shortly afterwards. Kosminski was the suspect, and after this identification which suspect knew, no other murder of this kind took place in London. Chief Inspector Donald Swanson.

The unfortunate man would appear to have been the individual who had assaulted Liz Stride outside the Working Men's Establishment, been recognised by Israel Schwartz, and detained by the police, but never charged or even called as a witness. Aaron Kosminski was confined to Colney Hatch Lunatic Asylum in 1888 until his death in 1919, not 'shortly afterwards' as claimed by Swanson.   Another wasted life, courtesy of Michael Maybrick.   Kosminski was no more guilty than Leather Apron, but was even more in the wrong place at the wrong time.   The fact that he was a Jewish immigrant would add further weight to the likelihood that he was the subject of Maybrick's utterance 'Lipski', and, fortunately for Michael Maybrick, Kosminski's detention may well have contributed to the otherwise inexplicable stepping down of the police presence in Whitechapel in late November 1889.

ON THE SQUARE

Mitre Square was not a typical London Square, but an enclosure of commercial buildings, dark and deserted at night, with three exits and well away from the usual haunt of prostitutes, indicative of a pre-arranged meeting, rather than a casual encounter, confirmed by the following observations in the Evening News.

Mitre Square is quite out off the beaten track, surrounded by warehouses and shops, and would be as deserted at midnight as though it lay in the centre of Salisbury Plain. No safer place, apparently, could possibly have been selected for the commission of such an awful crime, and the murderer, whoever he is, must have been familiar with that fact. It does not seem possible that accident could have led him to the spot so pre-eminently suited to its deadly purposes. The police, moreover, declare they have never known the place used for the purpose for which these wretched women court secrecy. Evening News. 1 October 1888.

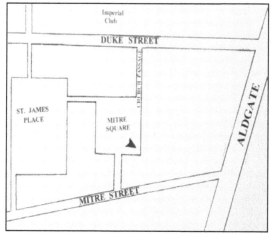

The pre-planned route to Mitre Square from King Street was an indirect line of alleyways, passages and courtyards, well-rehearsed in the daytime, and ready for the rendezvous. Mary Ann Kelly was about to learn the identity of the Whitechapel Murderer, as promised. The ensuing events were disclosed to a reporter from the Star newspaper by Constable Watkins, the officer patrolling the area around Mitre Square.

Sometimes I go into Mitre Square through the Church Passage, but last night I entered through Mitre Street. It was just half past one when I turned out of Aldgate and passed round the next corner into the Square. At that time there was nothing unusual to be seen. I looked carefully into all the corners as I always do.
                                                        The Star. 1 October 1888.

What Constable Watkins did not realise was that his movements had been watched and timed beforehand from outside the Square.

The policeman tramps by, as he has tramped before, and to those who have an interest in the calculation, his returning tread may be timed with the same certainty as the movements of a planetary body.   Daily News. 1 October 1888.

Announced well in advance by the sound of Constable Watkins' hob-nailed boots, his equally noisy departure from the Square would have been followed immediately by the appearance of the killer, very likely from the St. James Place passageway, never used by the police, following which, once the coast was clear, he would have called from within the Square to Mary Ann Kelly, already waiting opposite the Imperial Club near Church Passage. Anticipating a confidential disclosure by the trusted St. Jude's vigilante, Mary would have exchanged greetings and a friendly hug with her confidante, before being seized in a rear chokehold as the Whitechapel Murderer savoured the moment, the precipice of life and death, arms and legs flailing, body quivering, twitching, slumping. Euphoria. The madman's uncontrollable blood lust was then released in a frenzy of stabs, cuts and slashes, then away again by way of the covered passageway at the St. James's Place exit, heading north, then due east by way of Goulston Street. Constable Watkins continues his story, entering the Square from Mitre Street at around a quarter to two.

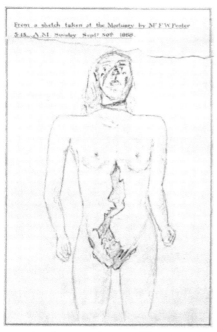

From a sketch taken at the Mortuary by Mr F W Foster 3.15. A.M. Sunday Sept 30th 1888.

I entered the Square by the same way. Here we are now at the entrance to the Square. I came this way, stopped at this corner to look up and down the street, and then turned in. As I came to the back of the picture frame makers, I turned my light into the corner, and there lay the woman. I can tell you, it didn't take me a moment to see that the Whitechapel Murderer had been our way. Her head lay here on this coal hole, and her clothes were thrown up breast high. The first thing that I noticed was that she was ripped up like a pig in the market. There was a big gash up the stomach, the entrails torn out and flung in a heap about her neck, with some of them lying in the ugly cut at the throat, and the face, well there was no face. Anyone who knew the woman alive would never recognise her by her face. I have been in the Force for a long while, but I never saw such a sight. The Star. October 1889.

On either cheek of the victim's face, had been deliberately carved an inverted letter 'V', unlike the other frenzied slashings, and seemingly a mysterious clue, with the link yet to be revealed.

The whore like all the rest was only too willing. The thrill she gave me was unlike all he others. I cut deep, deep, deep. Her nose annoyed me so I cut it off. Had a go at her eyes, left my mark. Diary of Jack the Ripper.

114

One of the doctors, in an interview with a Star reporter, after describing the various wounds, said the woman belonged to the very poorest class. She appeared to be an outcast, and carried her tea and sugar about with her. She was very thin. 'I should say from the fact that her hands were brown, that she had just come from the country, had been hop picking perhaps.'

The Star. 1 October 1888.

The inquest was held at the Coroner's Court, Golden Lane, on the 4th October under Coroner Samuel Langford, assisted by the City of London Solicitor, Henry Holmwood Crawford, on behalf of the police. Questions were addressed to Dr. Frederick Gordon Brown, Surgeon to the City of London Police, who carried out the inspection on the body immediately after the murder, assisted by Dr. George Bagster Phillips, who, although officially governed by the Metropolitan Police, was called in because of his familiarity with the Ripper's earlier victims. After describing in detail the extent of the horrific wounds, Dr. Brown added,

The uterus was cut away, and the left kidney was also cut out. Both these organs were absent, and have not been found. He must have had a good deal of knowledge of the abdominal organs, and the way to remove them. The work might have been done in five minutes, that is the least time it could have been done in.

Daily Telegraph. 4 October 1888.

The inquest continued, as witness Joseph Lawende testified,

Lawende: *I was at the Imperial Club, Duke Street, together with Mr. Levy and Mr. Harry Harris. It was raining, and we sat in the club till half-past one o'clock, when we left. I observed a man and woman together at the corner of Church Passage, Duke Street, leading to Mitre Square. The*

115

	woman was standing with her face towards the man, and I saw only her back. She had one hand on his breast. He was the taller. He had on a cloth cap with a peak of the same material.
Crawford:	*Unless the jury wish it, I do not think further particulars should be given as to the appearance of this man. Jury Foreman: The jury do not desire it.*
Coroner:	*Would you know him again?*
Lawende:	*I doubt it. The man and woman were about nine or ten feet away from me. It was half-past one o'clock when we rose to leave the club, and it would have been twenty five minutes to two o'clock when we passed the man and woman.*
Coroner:	*Did you overhear anything that either said?*
Lawende:	*No.*
Coroner:	*Did either appear in an angry mood?*
Lawende:	*No.*
Coroner:	*Did anything about their movements attract your attention?*
Lawende:	*No. The man looked rather rough and shabby.*
Coroner:	*When the woman placed her hand on the man's breast did she do it as if to push him away?*
Lawende	*No, it was done very quietly.*
Coroner:	*You were not curious enough to look back and see where they went?*
Lawende:	*No.*

Witness Joseph then testified,

Levy:	*I saw a man and a woman standing at the corner of Church Passage, but I did not take any notice of them.*

Coroner:	What height was the man?
Levy:	*I think he was three inches taller than the woman, who was perhaps five feet high. I cannot give any further description of them.*
Juryman:	*The point in the passage where the woman was standing was not well lighted?*
Levy:	*On the contrary, I think it was badly lighted then, but the light is much better now.*

Henry Holmwood Crawford was at pains to withhold Lawende's description of the man seen in Church Passage, but nevertheless Joseph Levy had volunteered that the man was around five feet three inches in height. Six weeks later, a report was published in the Daily Telegraph.

A correspondent forwards copies of the descriptions of certain men who were last seen in the company of the woman who was mutilated in Mitre Square. These authentic descriptions, we have reason to know, have been secretly circulated by the authorities of Scotland Yard since October 26th, but the complete details have never been made public. The point which the police appear to have been at most pains to suppress is the significant one that the unknown murderer has the 'appearance of a sailor'. At 1.35 am, 30th September, in Church Passage, leading to Mitre Square, where she was found murdered at 1.45 am, same date, a man aged 30, height five feet seven or eight inches, complexion fair, moustache fair, medium build, dress, pepper and salt colour, loose jacket, grey cloth cap, reddish handkerchief tied in knot, appearance of a sailor.   Daily Telegraph. 12 November 1888.

According to these police reports, the suspect had grown in height from five feet three inches, as testified on oath by Joseph Levy at the inquest, to five feet eight inches. In reality, whoever the witnesses saw that night, there is every likelihood that the man at the corner of Church Passage was indeed a sailor. Mary Ann Kelly was a prostitute, and sailors seem irresistibly attracted to prostitutes, particularly the only one around, and to all appearances, in this instance, the man's advances were being politely declined. Mary was awaiting a pressing appointment with someone else.

Of all the facts regarding events in Mitre Square, the one absolute certainty is the man seen on the corner of Church Passage whilst men were leaving the nearby Imperial Club, was definitely not the murderer, particularly after the close encounter he had just experienced with Liz Stride outside another working men's club, less than one hour previously. Michael Maybrick was there already, unseen, lurking in the dark shadows of the Square, ready to share with Mary Ann Kelly the identity of the Whitechapel Murderer.

Bro. Dr. Gordon Brown, City of London Police Surgeon, was a member of the Savage Club, and Savage Club Lodge No.2190, having been elected in 1887 as Grand Steward of the United Grand Lodge of England. Neither he nor Bro. Henry Holmwood Crawford, City of London Solicitor, of Alliance Lodge No.1827, had the slightest clue of the identity of the Mitre Square murderer, but their Masonic colleague Bro. Michael Maybrick was very familiar with his identity, a source of great personal amusement whenever they met.

The terror of Whitechapel has walked again, and this time has marked down two victims, one hacked and disfigured beyond discovery, the other with the throat cut and torn. Again he has got away clear, and again the police, with wonderful frankness, confess that they have not got a clue. Granting that he has some rough knowledge of anatomy, it is probable that his hands only would be smeared by his bloody work, and after the deed he would put on gloves. He must have done so to ensnare the second woman. As he nowhere stays to wash his hands, he probably does not inhabit lodging houses or hotels, but a private house where he has facilities, perhaps a hand-wash stand communicating directly with a pipe, for getting rid of bloody hands. He must be inoffensive, probably respectable in manner and appearance, or else after the murderous warnings of last week, woman after woman could not have been decoyed by him.

.   The Star. 1 October 1888.

The Funny Little Game was over. Liz Stride was an unintended victim, an unavoidable nuisance and one whore less on the streets, but not part of this carefully orchestrated plan. Mary Ann Kelly, possessing the required 'MA' factor, had obligingly provided the letter 'K' to complete his name. Divine retribution, at the behest of Michael Maybrick.

MARTHA_ TABRAM	**M**HA** MA*BR*****
MARY_ ANN NICHOLS	**MICHA*L MAYBR*****
ANNIE CHAPMAN	**MICHAEL MAYBRIC***
MARY ANN KELLY	**MICHAEL MAYBRICK**

THE WRITING ON THE WALL

Mary Ann Kelly's throat had been cut, stomach sliced open, intestines ripped out and thrown over her shoulder, a triangle carved on each cheek, and the uterus and one kidney removed. Half of Mary's apron had been sliced off, with the bloodstained item found next to a door entrance in Goulston Street, en route from Mitre Square to the rear access gate in Wentworth Street.

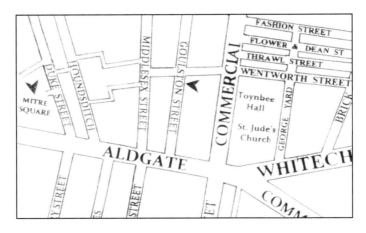

Just why the apron section was cut away and removed has never been fully addressed, but there is a very plausible explanation. The cloth was used to wrap up and convey the bloody and slippery kidney and uterus as far as the temporary stop in Goulston Street, by which time absorption into the cloth had rendered the items sufficiently manageable, and the apron was then unceremoniously dumped, a clear indication of the killer's escape route, and potentially a serious error of judgment. Once back within the jurisdiction of the Metropolitan Police, Maybrick just could not resist leaving a tease for the Commissioner. Scribbled on the wall in the door entrance was the seemingly illiterate phrase, 'The Juwes are the men that will not be blamed for nothing', in tailor's chalk, from an empty room in King Street.

On the fair assumption that there was a connection between the writing and the apron, at first sight it would seem the assassin was exonerating from blame anyone associated with the Jewish Working Men's Club in Berner Street, unplanned as the Liz Stride murder had been, and it is likely that the deranged narcissist was intent on claiming the kill. The case has also been argued that the spelling of the word 'Juwes' has a Masonic significance, which merits further consideration.

LIGHT ON MASONRY:

A COLLECTION OF ALL THE

MOST IMPORTANT DOCUMENTS

ON THE SUBJECT OF

SPECULATIVE FREE MASONRY:

WITH

ALL THE DEGREES OF THE ORDER CONFERRED IN A MASTER'S LODGE, ALL THE DEGREES CONFERRED IN THE ROYAL ARCH CHAPTER AND GRAND EN- CAMPMENT OF KNIGHTS TEMPLARS, WITH THE APPENDANT ORDERS,

As published by the Convention of Seceding Masons, held at Le Roy, July 4th and 5th, 1828.

In 1829, Freemason David Bernard wrote a treatise entitled 'Light on Masonry. A Collection of all the Most Important Documents on the Subject of Speculative Freemasonry.' In this work, reference is made to a trio of ruffians, who, on being captured following their murder of the legendary Masonic character Hiram Abiff, exclaimed as follows,

Jubela: Oh that my throat had been cut across....
Jubelo: Oh that my left breast had been torn open, and my heart and vitals taken there from, and thrown over my left shoulder....
Jubelum: Oh that my body had been cut in two in the midst ....

121

The three were duly punished in accordance with the grisly manner of their requests. Some claim the chalked word 'Juwes' refers to these characters, inferring the deliberately selected Whitechapel victims were mutilated in a manner similar to the old Masonic tradition, the words of which were still used in contemporary Masonic ritual, and would have been familiar to Freemasons at the time of the murders. Further reference is made in Barnard's book to part of the Masonic initiation ceremony, when the candidate is asked, 'How were you prepared', to which the response is 'I was divested of all metals', which evidently includes rings and coins. Although the victims were poor prostitutes, not one coin was found on any of the bodies, and all rings had been removed. Herewith the similarities,

Martha Tabram	Throat cut across.
Mary Ann Nichols	Throat cut across.
	Deep cuts across the abdomen.
	Impression of missing ring on finger.
Annie Chapman	Throat cut across.
	Deep cuts to abdomen, intestines placed on right shoulder.
	Metal rings removed and missing.
Liz Stride (unplanned)	Throat cut across.
	No marks to body.
Mary Ann Kelly	Throat cut across.
	Deep cuts to abdomen, intestines placed on right shoulder.
	Womb and left kidney removed.

Was another Funny Little Game being played alongside the first? Every Freemason in the land would have been avidly following the press releases after the debacle over Leather Apron, and the disturbing possibility of a Masonic connection must have been discussed at many a Lodge meeting. Unsurprisingly, when police records were released one hundred years after the event, not one reference to Freemasonry was found, nor indeed was any such suggestion ever raised in the national press at the time.

Berner Street and Goulston Street were under the governance of the Metropolitan Police, whilst Mitre Square fell just outside the jurisdiction of the Metropolitan Police, under control of the autonomous City of London Police. If confusion within the police ranks was Michael Maybrick's intention, then the plan succeeded, as the Met was effectively locked out of the Mitre Square investigation. The Goulston Street graffiti was in the Metropolitan area, but had been discovered by the City Police, who, although off territory in their search, dutifully guarded the site, awaiting arrival of the Metropolitan Police and police photographer. However, on being notified of the ongoing events early that morning, Sir Charles Warren headed, not for the murder scene at Berner Street, but straight to the graffiti at Goulston Street. Why give priority to a chalked message rather than the dead body in Berner Street? What happened next effectively sealed Bro. Charles Warren's fate as Chief of the Metropolitan Police, as summed up in the following article.

The murderer, after killing the victim in Mitre Square within the City boundaries, seems to have gone down Goulston Street, which is outside the city boundary, and under the jurisdiction of Sir Charles Warren. Here the murderer threw away a portion of the murdered woman's apron, after wiping his hands. On the wall in close proximity to the place where the bloody apron was found, there was written up the following inscription, 'The Juwes shall not be blamed for nothing.' The inscription was subsequently erased, it was supposed by some stupid blunder. It is now stated that the erasure was made by the express orders of Sir Charles Warren, who personally superintended the operation. The City Police attached the greatest value to this clue, and decided to have the inscription photographed. The City Police were taking the most obvious of precautions by arranging to have it photographed, and they stationed one of their own officers in Goulston Street, although it was outside their district, to see that no one tampered with the inscription. Unfortunately, they reckoned without Sir Charles Warren. The Chief Commissioner himself visited the spot, saw the inscription, and at once gave orders for its removal. It was in vain for the City officer to protest, as he had no jurisdiction in the Metropolitan Police District. The Pall Mall Gazette. 11 October 1888.

According to official sources, the removal of the writing was explained away by Sir Charles Warren as having been necessary to prevent a riot against the local Jewish population. No explanation, however, was forthcoming as to why the writing was not simply covered over, to await the arrival of the police photographer. Brother Charles Warren was well and truly convinced that the Whitechapel Murderer was a fellow Freemason, and the first parties with whom he liaised, deeply involved in the Mitre Square investigation, would have been Freemasons Bro. Frederick Gordon Brown, City of London Police Surgeon, and Bro. Henry Holmwood Crawford, City of London Solicitor and Public Prosecutor. All were mystified, and uncertain as to the inferences, but one thing was certain, the press were not prepared to let the matter rest, relentlessly ridiculing the Commissioner as incompetent, much to the delight of Michael Maybrick. The Funny Little Game was complete, the creation of Michael Maybrick's own name from those of his victims, the manifestation of revenge, conceived and formulated by a brilliant, deviant psychopath. Not only was the anagram complete, but other nuances were also being played out, including a cryptic message to his masonic adversary Bro. Sir Charles Warren, in the form of that most ancient of Masonic

symbols, the triangle, often displaying the all-seeing eye, as on the dollar note of the USA, where the Declaration of Independence in 1776 was signed by ten Freemasons, including Benjamin Franklin, Grand Master of Pennsylvania.

The murder sites of the specifically selected victims, excluding the unintentional victim Liz Stride, were as follows,

Annie Chapman   Hanbury Street

Mary Ann Nichols   Buck's Row

Mary Jane Kelly   Mitre Square

The sites not only form a neat triangle, but the base line passes clean through George Yard, where Martha Tabram met her fate, and incredibly, over half of the letters in each site name form the basis, not only for Maybrick, but 'Br. Maybrick', a last wave of defiance to Bro. Sir Charles Warren.

h A n B u R Y	ABRY	
B u C K s	BCK	
M I t R e	MIR	BR. MAYBRICK

If further proof were required to conclusively confirm the name of

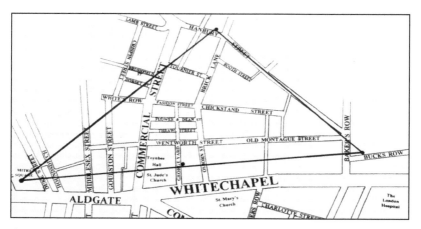

the master cryptologist behind this conundrum, simply enlarge 'Buck's' into 'Buck's Row'...

HA n B u RY   **HABRY**

B u CKs   RO w   **BCKRO**

MITRE   **MITRE**   **BROTHER MAYBRICK**

Only four of the twenty letters were unused. Just when do a series of unlikely 'coincidences' cease to be coincidence, and constitute deliberately contrived, indisputable facts? This is the work of an intellectual genius, proving beyond doubt that none of these murders were spontaneous. In each case, both victim and site had been clinically and meticulously selected to comply with the constraints of the Funny Little Game, revealing a depth of forward planning and an intensity of purpose almost beyond belief.

Michael Maybrick would have been ecstatic at the success of the venture. He had wreaked revenge on the whore by extracting his name from the souls of the lookalike victims, and had left a message for Sir Charles Warren that a Freemason was responsible, ending the Funny Little Game with a neat triangle, finishing 'On the Square'. Maybrick's incredible self-belief was epitomised by the blatant anagrams of his own name, testimony to his invincibility, protected by his guardian angels. He was invisible, totally in control of a reign of terror on the streets of London, and trumpeted by the press as the most dangerous, elusive, and enigmatic man in the land.

His euphoria, however, was to be short lived. Doubts were being expressed over the real name of the Mitre Square victim.

The police are proceeding with the task of securing a complete identification of the woman Kelly. Her sister was found at her home in Thrawl Street, and had no difficulty identifying the body. She said that she had not seen the deceased for a long time, and had no knowledge that she was known by the name of Kelly.
The Star. 3 October 1888.

It was soon established that the real name of the second victim of the night was not Kelly, a name adopted for respectability whilst living with long term partner John Kelly, as testified at the inquest.

I am deputy of the lodging house at Flower and Dean Street. I have known the deceased and Kelly during the last seven years. They passed as man and wife, and lived on very good terms.
inquest testament. Frederick Williamson.

Known as Kate Kelly whilst living with John Kelly, the victim evidently changed names as and when it suited, a practice not uncommon amongst women of this profession. Within days, it was established that the victim's real name was Catherine Eddowes. Stride and Eddowes had been murdered unnecessarily, but that was of no consequence, an annoying inconvenience. Two wasted lives mattered not. The search would go on for the elusive missing letter 'K', needed to complete the still ongoing Funny Little Game.

REWARD AND SPECULATION

Ironically, the day after Mary Ann Kelly had been lured to her death by the prospect of a £100 reward, the City of London Police Commissioner, Sir James Fraser, declared a police reward of £500, followed four days later by an announcement by the Lord Mayor of London, Polydor de Kayser, of an additional £500 from the City of London. Notwithstanding the whole of Whitechapel being in panic mode over the atrocities, the intelligence division of the Met next embarked on an inspirational course of action. Handbills were posted on the door of every household, advising that a series of murders had recently been committed in Whitechapel, and asking for details of any suspicious characters, lest the thought had not already occurred to the traumatised residents of the area.

Shock waves reverberated around the community as word spread of the double murder, and an air of despondency fell over the soup kitchens, as the poorest of the poor continued to struggle for survival.

POLICE NOTICE.

TO THE OCCUPIER.

On the mornings of Friday, 31st August, Saturday 8th, and Sunday, 30th September, 1888, Women were murdered in or near Whitechapel, supposed by some one residing in the immediate neighbourhood. Should you know of any person to whom suspicion is attached, you are earnestly requested to communicate at once with the nearest Police Station.

Metropolitan Police Office,
30th September 1888

Printed by M'Corquodale & Co. Limited — The Armoury — Southwark

The door opened into a large room. The walls were black with grime and filth, the floor was inches deep with dirt, and the atmosphere could have been served up with a spoon. On the benches and tables sat or squatted some half a hundred men and

128

women of all ages and degrees of poverty. A huge fireplace at the end of the room held a cooking apparatus, on which were displayed a score of suppers in course of preparation, and there, in a halo of vile vapour and amid an incense of fried fish, stood One-Armed Liz. She had known Liz Stride well. She was sorry she was dead, but would be glad if Liz's death would lead to the capture of that butcher. Then along came a woman with an armful of walking sticks, showing each one that they were swordsticks, of a cheap but dangerous pattern. 'Here you are now,' she cried 'Sixpence for a swordstick.' She does good business in Berner Street and has sold a lot of them.

.   The Star. 1 October 1888.

The Metropolitan Police 'H' Division, with a complement of 548 men, covered Whitechapel at the time of the early murders, but as the workload increased, it was found necessary to draft in Scotland Yard. Sir Charles Warren had appointed Robert Anderson as Assistant Commissioner, but immediately after the Annie Chapman murder Anderson left for Switzerland on sick leave, giving rise to controversy over Warren's judgemental capability. Anderson's arrogance and blatant disregard for the responsibility of his office is epitomised in his memoirs, written twenty years later.

I was at that time physically unfit to enter on the duties of my new post. I told Mr. Matthews, greatly to his distress, that I could not take up my duties until I had had a month's holiday in Switzerland, and so, after one week at Scotland Yard, I crossed the Channel. The second of the crimes known as the Whitechapel murders was committed the night before I took office, and the third occurred the night of the day on which I left London. The newspapers soon began to comment on my absence, and letters from Whitehall decided me to spend the last week of my holiday in Paris, that I might be in touch with my office. On the night of my arrival in Paris, two more victims fell to the knife of the murder fiend. Next day's post bought me an urgent appeal from Mr.

Matthews to return to London, and of course I complied. On my
return I found the Jack the Ripper scare in full swing. When the
stolid English go for a scare, they take leave of all moderation
and common sense.

The Lighter Side of my Official Life. Sir Robert Anderson. 1910.

The Superintendent of 'H' Division was Thomas Arnold, but he
too went on sick leave after the double murder of Stride and
Eddowes. Given these splendid examples of leadership, the press
had a field day. It was now obvious that a dangerous serial killer
was at large, able to appear from nowhere, vanish from the scene
of the crime, and, more ominously, blend amongst the general
public of Whitechapel, whilst those in charge of the investigations
opted to take time off work. Speculation continued as to who the
murderer could be, with suggestions submitted to the newspapers
including slaughterman, doctor, medical student, vagrant, soldier,
sailor, the list went on and on. A particularly interesting letter was
forwarded to the editor of the Evening News.

Sir,

I ask you to allow me to quote the facts of a case which came
under my observing some years ago. I had a young friend who
had just returned home from college, and whose parents resided
in the country. He was a fine, handsome young fellow, and his
parents were very proud of him. After he had been home a few
weeks, he received an invitation to visit some friends in London.
While on this visit, being young and easily beguiled, he
contracted a disease. When he returned home, he confided his
secret to me, and I entreated him to see a medical man at once but
he would not do so. Things went on in this way for nearly a year,
and instead of getting better, he got worse. For about every
three weeks he would become morose, and his whole thoughts
were concentrated on murder. He informed me that the woman
from whom he had contracted the disease was 22 years of age,
and it is a singular thing that, although his whole animosity was
confined to women-kind, he never attempted to injure a middle

130

aged lady, but if his sisters, aged 20 and 22, came near him, he would fly at them like a tiger and curse them, swearing they had been his ruin. It was just the same if he saw young ladies of that age. At last, dangerous symptoms began to develop themselves, passing along the street. He would snatch up a knife, or any other weapon he could get hold of, and swear he would murder them. He had a delusion that they were all prostitutes, and that he had a mission to murder them wholesale, and yet, when he recovered from this mania, he was quite unconscious of his acts, and would be as affectionate and as gentle to his sisters and their young lady friends as if nothing unusual had happened. While the mania was strong upon him, he showed astounding cunning, and had to be watched day and night, or there is no doubt he would have murdered his victims by wholesale slaughter. At last he became worse, and one day he attacked his favourite sister, injuring her so severely that his friends were compelled to placed him in a lunatic asylum. .   Evening News. 6 October 1888.

A classic example of the early onset of neurosyphilis, whilst that exhibited by Michael Maybrick had lain dormant for almost thirty years, only triggered by close contact with prostitutes, coinciding with his arrival at Toynbee Hall, in the heart of the most notorious part of Whitechapel, where prostitution was rife. The correspondent continues by making a remarkably astute observation.

Now, sir, I am not a medical man, but with your kind permission I would like to point out a similarity between this case and the monster now committing the atrocious crimes in our midst. Is it not singular that the whole of the unfortunate women butchered in Whitechapel are about the same age, from 35 to 45? Can it be possible that this fiend has suffered the same way as my friend, and has sworn a deadly revenge against all unfortunates of that age? I see that the police are making vigorous searches in the lodging houses of Whitechapel. I wonder if they have thought it possible that the assassin may have taken refuge in one of the

vaults of the churches in that neighbourhood? One thing is certain, they need not look for him in lodging houses.
.   Evening News. 6 October. 1888.

The suggestion appears to have been ignored by the ever vigilant Whitechapel police. The Rev. Samuel Barnett hadn't the slightest clue that he was secretly harbouring the Whitechapel Murderer, and so impressed was he by his new found friend that the following year, he was inspired to write the following article in the Toynbee Journal.

Organ recitals on Saturday afternoons are an established institution at St. Jude's, Kensington. Eminent organists like Dr. Bridge, of Westminster Abbey, or Mr. C. H. Lloyd of Christ Church Cathedral, Oxford, are invited to give them. There is no reason why such recitals should not be equally an institution at St. Jude's, Whitechapel. The crowds who flock to hear Oratories in our church, and those who came Sunday after Sunday to the Organ Recital at the People's Palace, are proof that there is no lack of love for good music in East London.   Toynbee Journal. 1889.

Something had inspired this pattern of thought. Perhaps Michael Maybrick had assured the Rev. Barnett of a personal appearance, although there is no record in the Toynbee Journal of that ever having taken place. The good clergyman kept his part of the arrangement, with not a word mentioned of their innocuous private pact, never realising that St. Jude's Church, with its surreal pictorial overtones, was serving as the base for the Whitechapel Murderer.

JACK THE RIPPER

Prior to the double event on the night of the 30th September, a letter dated the 25th September had been received on the 27th at the Central News Agency in Fleet Street, signed 'Jack the Ripper', and requesting 'Keep this letter back until I do a bit more work, then give it out straight', which is exactly what the recipients did, by disregarding the letter in the belief that it was a prank.

Dear Boss,
I keep on hearing the police have caught me, but they won't fix me just yet. I have laughed when they look so clever, and talk about being on the right track. That joke about Leather Apron gave me real fits. I am down on whores and I shan't quit ripping them till I do get buckled. Great work the last job was. I gave the lady no time to squeal. How can they catch me now? I love my work and want to start again. You will soon hear of me with my Funny Little Games. I saved some of the proper red stuff in a ginger beer bottle over the last job, to write with, but it went thick like glue and I can't use it. Red ink is fit enough I hope, ha, ha. The next job I do I shall clip the ladies ears off and send to the police officers just for jolly, wouldn't you. Keep this letter back until I do a bit more work, then give it out straight. My knife is nice and sharp I want to get to work right away if I get a chance. Good luck.
Yours truly,
Jack the Ripper. Don't mind me giving the trade name.

The letter oozes Michael Maybrick. Leather Apron was detested by the general public, but Maybrick found the Masonic inference hilarious. The 'Funny Little Games' were a source of personal pride which could no longer be contained and just had to be flaunted to the masses, despite no one having a clue as to the meaning. The thrill was mounting, the tension overwhelming,

133

25. Sept. 1888.

Dear Boss

        I keep on hearing the police
have caught me. but they wont fix
me just yet. I have laughed when
they look so clever and talk about
being on the right track. That joke
about Leather apron gave me real
fits. I am down on whores and
I shant quit ripping them till I
do get buckled. Grand work the last
job was, I gave the lady no time to
squeal How can they catch me now.
I love my work and want to start
again. you will soon hear of me
with my funny little games. I
saved some of the proper red stuff in
a ginger beer bottle over the last job
to write with but it went thick
like glue and I cant use it. Red
ink is fit enough I hope ha. ha.
The next job I do I shall clip
the ladys ears off and send to the

police officers just for jolly wouldnt
you. Keep this letter back till I
do a bit more work. then give
it out straight My knife's so nice
and sharp I want to get to work
right away if I get a chance.
Good luck.
           yours truly
             Jack the Ripper
Dont mind me giving the trade name

134

but the lack of adulation was unbearable. He yearned desperately to share his success with the world, without actually revealing his identity. Further mischief was imminent. Four years earlier, Michael Maybrick had celebrated the success of his singalong ballad 'They all Love Jack' which had soon been adopted as the regimental march of the 20th Middlesex (Artists) Rifles.

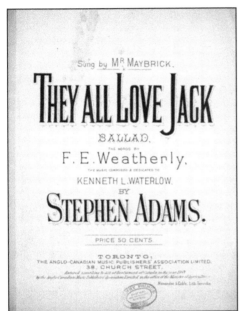

The Regimental March 'They All Love Jack' was a composition of one of our celebrated officers of later years, Capt. Michael Maybrick, who wrote under the name of Stephen Adams, and was adopted by the corps as their regimental march in the 80's.

Col. H.R.A. May. Memories of the (Artists) Rifles.

Perfect. Jack the Ripper it would be. Everyone was humming the tune, Michael Maybrick's grand finale at every concert.

'Jack' had become his trade name, but the fools would never guess the link with the Ripper letter. How very clever. The letter was a declaration of bravado, a boast of his success to the public at large. The Central News Agency withheld the letter, then, on 1st October, a postcard was received, again signed 'Jack the Ripper'.

I was not codding, dear old Boss, when I gave you the tip, you'll hear of Saucy Jacky's work tomorrow. Double event this time, number one squealed a bit, could not finish straight off. Had no time to get ears for police, thanks for keeping last letter back until I got to work again. Jack the Ripper.

The content and timing left no doubt that the same hand had written both letter and postcard, but there was a notable variation in the handwriting, which serves well to indicate the inconsistencies which would be manifested in future communications. Note, however, the similarity between the articulate letter 'B' on the second line, and the 'B' in 'Dear Boss'. (p.134). Also the 'J' in Jacky,' on the fifth, with the 'J' in 'Jack' in the signature on the same Dear Boss letter.

Of additional significance, the postcard inadvertently contained a link to the tall stranger in Berner Street. Received the day after the murders of Liz Stride and Mary Ann Kelly, the postcard refers to 'double event this time, number one squealed a bit, couldn't finish straight off', which tallies exactly with known events in Berner Street the night before. Liz Stride was the only victim who had seen trouble coming, and it was on record that Liz Stride had screamed when assaulted earlier, very likely sounding off again when confronted by her killer, revealing the content of the postcard to be disconcertingly close to the known, but as yet undisclosed, facts of Liz Stride's last moments.

Israel Schwartz had yet to give his account to the police and the press, and there were only two other living witnesses, one of whom was detained by the police, and the other the tall stranger, author of both letter and postcard. In no time at all, press attention ensured that the Whitechapel Murderer metamorphosed into Jack the Ripper, and the legend was born. Michael Maybrick was centre stage again.

American journalist George R. Sims, an avid follower of the events in Whitechapel, added his own take on the subject.

Jack the Ripper is the hero of the hour. A gruesome wag, a grim practical joker, has succeeded in getting an enormous amount of fun out of a postcard which he sent to the Central News. The fun is all his own, and nobody shares with it, but he must be gloating demonically as the state of perturbation in which he has flung the public. George R. Sims. The Referee. 7 October 1888.

On the 4th October, when a facsimile of the 'Dear Boss' letter appeared in the Evening News, the handwriting came to be regarded as the benchmark in appraising the authorship of subsequent Ripper letters, nearly all of which were hoaxes, leading to a considerable degree of misdirection. To add to the growing apprehension within Whitechapel as the murders continued unabated, another grisly discovery was made on the 1st October inside the vaults of the New Scotland Yard Headquarters, Whitehall, then in the early stages of construction.

The horrible find was made in the new police buildings between Parliament Street and the Embankment. The corpse was a mere trunk, both head and limbs having been severed in an apparently brutal and unskilful manner. Evidently, the trunk was that of a young and healthy woman. The head has undoubtedly been sawn off in this case, and the same instrument was apparently used in taking off the legs. The difficulty and danger which the murderer must have encountered on bearing the body to its hiding place increases the mystery. It is on the site of what was intended for the National Opera House, that the new central police buildings are being erected. The place in which the trunk was found was such an out of the way kind that one is led to the conclusion that it was deposited there by some party acquainted with the building. But one avenue of approach existed, and that was from the obscure corner of the north end of Cannon Row, a seven foot hoarding. It would be a very heavy and clumsy parcel to carry for any distance, and in the second place, it seems doubtful if it was sufficiently concealed to have been carried far, without incurring great risk. The skirt in which it was wrapped appeared to have been brought up as far as it would go, but the breasts apparently had never been covered by the skirt. It could never have been carried through the streets in that partially covered manner. The Star. 3 October 1888.

Whilst the crime displays none of the usual characteristics of the Whitechapel Murders, the likelihood cannot be dismissed that Michael Maybrick would have been drawn to the construction of the new National Opera House, in which he would one day appear, plans for which had been abandoned at vault level, where the corpse was found. Was he indeed familiar with the layout of the vaults in the building where he believed he would be starring one day? On the 5th October, the Central News Agency received another communication purporting to come from the Ripper, although on this occasion journalist Tom Bulling took it upon himself to forward to Chief Inspector Adolphus Williamson of the Metropolitan Police, not the original letter, but a transcript of the letter in his own handwriting, accompanied by the original envelope and a covering note. Just why Tom Bulling kept the original letter remains a mystery.

138

Dear Mr. Williamson,

At 5 minutes to 9 o' clock tonight we received the following letter, the envelope of which I enclose, by which you will see it is in the same handwriting as the previous communications.

Yours truly,   T.J. Bulling

In the name of God hear me.   I swear I did not kill the female whose body was found at Whitehall.   If she was an honest woman I will hunt down and destroy the murderer.   If she was a whore God bless the hand that slew her, for the women of Moab and Midian shall die and their blood shall mingle with the dust.   I never harm any others, or the Divine Power that protects and helps me in my grand work would quit forever.   Do as I do and the light of glory shall shine upon you.   I must get to work tomorrow, treble event this time.   Yes, yes, three must be ripped. Will dear old Boss.   The police now reckon my work a practical joke, well, well, Jacky's a very practical joker ha, ha, ha, keep this back until three are wiped out and you can show the cold meat.

Yours truly   Jack the Ripper.

Maybrick had soon learned that Mary Ann Kelly was really Catherine Eddowes, and he was not at all pleased.   The whole night had been a complete waste of time at considerable personal risk, added to which he had been seen at the Liz Stride murder site by Schwartz and the assailant.   Insinuations within the press that the Whitehall torso may have been the work of the Whitechapel Murderer had caused further upset, hence the Ripper's letter of denial.   Association with the torso would upset the letter sequence of the 'Funny Little Games' and had to be discounted, almost as a personal affront.

As with the 'Dear Boss' letter, the content exudes Michael Maybrick through and through.   The women of Moab and Midian refer to Aholah and Aholiba, whores straight from Chapter 23 of the Book of Ezekiel. 'The Divine power that protects and helps me in my grand work' is the personification of Maybrick's guardian angel, identified with Ezekiel. The 'treble event' and 'till three are wiped out' were not predictions of three more murders, but obtuse references to the next victim being allocated as the third of a trio, incorporating the last two unnecessary kills, which had already spoilt the sequence of letters in the Funny Little Game. Three become one, which was perfectly justifiable in Michael Maybrick's mindset, ensuring continuity in the Funny Little Game, regardless of this minor setback.

The ever astute George R. Sims makes a very pertinent observation regarding the ongoing influence of Ezekiel behind Michael Maybrick's behavioural pattern.

Perhaps he is a butcher whose mind is affected by the changes of the moon, and who had been much impressed by the reading of Ezekiel Chapter 23. The Chapter refers to the vicious lives of the sisters Aholah and Aholiba, and verse 25 is the key to the situation. 'And I will set my jealousy against thee, and they shall deal furiously with thee, they shall take away thy nose and thy ears; and thy remnant shall fall by the sword.' Verse 48 sums up the case, 'Thus will cause lewdness to cease out of the land, that all women may be taught not to do after your lewdness.' This theory, which for purpose of reference may be called 'the Ezekiel theory' is as probably as near to the mark of any of the 'guesses of truth' which have been plentiful of late. A new murder is confidently anticipated by the Vigilance Committee, and extraordinary precautions have been taken to prevent the man who has taken the Book of Ezekiel too literally, walking away again. The Referee. 2 December 1888.

A new murder was certainly on the mind of one particular member of St. Jude's Vigilance Association, but there still remained the nagging problem of the witnesses who had seen him at the murder site in Berner Street. The following letter, dated the 6th October, is on police files.

You thought yourself very clever I reckon when you informed the police. But you made a mistake if you thought I didn't see you. Now I know you know me, and I see your little game, I mean to finish you and send your ears to your wife if you show this to the police or help them, if you do I will finish you. It is no use you trying to get out of my way, because I have you when you don't expect it and I keep my word as you soon see and rip you up.
Yours truly

Jack the Ripper.

The letter was not addressed to any named person, but was clearly intended by the real murderer to appear as though sent by

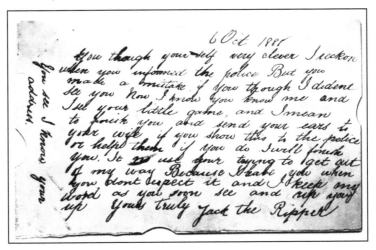

the man seen scuffling with Liz Stride, to implicate him further. The intended recipient remains unknown, but someone had handed the letter to the police, and had it been Schwartz or Packer, he would have suffered a succession of sleepless nights.

Whether or not Inspector Abberline was fooled by the deception is a matter for conjecture, but note the similarity in signature with that in the 'Dear Boss' letter. (p.134). Also the distinctive letter 'B'.

For the previous few days, Michael Maybrick had been fuming inwardly at the transcribing of his letter by Tom Bulling, and on the 10th October 1888, he wrote a letter, postmarked Edinburgh, to the City Police, subsequently forwarded on the 11th October to the Metropolitan Police.

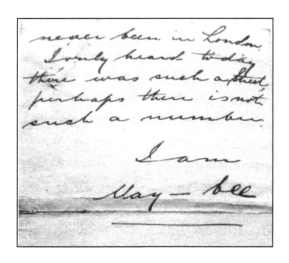

Dear Sir,

I beg to inform you that I have been impressed for three days with the thought that the Whitechapel Murderer is living at 29 Fleet Street, London. This is merely supposition in my part, for I do not know him. Further, I have never been in London. I only heard today that there was such a street, perhaps there is not such a number.

I am, May-bee.

The letter is a jumble of nonsense and denials, pointing the finger at a journalist in Fleet Street, but the reckless signature, 'May-bee', may just as well have read 'Maybrick, Toynbee'. Caution had been thrown to the wind in a spontaneous act of self-assertion, to correct the record, regain control, and discredit the upstart journalist who was usurping his achievements. Michael Maybrick was an extremely intelligent man, composer of classical scores, and very possibly a chess master, but he had been uncharacteristically stupid in allowing his monstrous ego to push the 'Funny Little Game' to its limits. He regarded himself as invincible, but the rash 'May-bee' signature could have rendered him very vulnerable indeed.

Ripper letters had been received by the score from a number of sources after the publication of the 'Dear Boss' letter, penned by persons intent on sowing confusion in the ranks of the now ridiculed police. Only a small number appear genuine, mischievously penned in a variety of writing styles, as readily instanced by the differing scripts in the 'Dear Boss' letter and associated postcard, irrefutably connected by content, written by the same hand, but in different styles. In the case of the 'May-bee' letter, Michael Maybrick's guard had definitely dropped, due perhaps to the partaking of nectar from the local Edinburgh distillery. Most, if not all, of his publicity signatures are in the name of Stephen Adams, and Maybrick signatures are rare, but two are present on the 1911 National Census, the first of which requiring the registration form to be completed by the head of the household. There is a distinct similarity in 'May' of both Maybrick names in the census, and the 'May' in 'Maybee', almost identical, and yet another link between Michael Maybrick and a Ripper letter.

Interestingly, also worthy of note is the variation between the letter 'S' in 'Slingo' and 'Servant', written in succession on the

1	Michael Maybrick	Head
2	Laura Maybrick	Wife
3	Edith Slinge	Servant
4	Nellie Gordon	Servant
5	Alice Tivier	Servant

same line, exemplifying the subconscious differences in handwriting emanating from the hand of Michael Maybrick. Fortunately, police and press attention was focused elsewhere, and seemingly neither paid the 'May-bee' letter any attention, being filed away and forgotten for over 130 years, although not before having spent some time on the desk of Detective Inspector Frederick Abberline.

S.E. MIBRAC

On the 9th October 1888, an article was published in The Globe, a relatively low circulation London newspaper, recounting the story of a mysterious stranger having left behind a black leather bag in a well-known first class London West End Hotel. The bag contained wearing apparel, cheque books, letters and 'prints of an obscene nature.' The article, provided by a mysterious 'undeniably authentic', but totally anonymous source, refers to the man having recently journeyed to Liverpool, where his movements, being 'of a mysterious kind,' were being closely followed by members of the CID. Two days after appearing in the Globe, an identical article was published in the Liverpool Daily Post.

THE EAST-END MURDERS.

A STRANGE STORY.

DETECTIVES ON A NEW SCENT.

A well-informed correspondent states that he has gleaned the following information from an undeniably authentic source, and from careful and persistent inquiries in various quarters he is able to relate the news as fact, though for obvious reasons names and addresses are for the present suppressed: —A certain member of the Criminal Investigation Department has recently journeyed to Liverpool and there traced the movements of a man which have proved of a somewhat mysterious kind. The height of this person and his description generally are fully ascertained, and among other things he was in possession of a black leather bag. This man suddenly left Liverpool for London, and for some time occupied apartments in a well-known first-class hotel in the West-end. It is stated that for some reason or another this person was in the habit of "slumming;" he would visit the lowest parts of London, and scour the slums of the East-end. He suddenly disappeared from the hotel leaving behind the black leather bag and its contents, and has not returned. He left a small bill unpaid, and ultimately an advertisement appeared in the *Times*, setting forth the gentleman's name, and drawing attention to the fact that the bag would be sold under the innkeepers' Act to defray expenses, unless claimed. This was done last month by a well known auctioneer in London, and the contents, or some of them, are now in the possession of the police, who are thoroughly investigating the affair. Of these we, of course, cannot more than make mention, but certain documents, wearing apparel, cheque books, prints of an obscene description, letters, &c., are said to form the foundation of a most searching inquiry now on foot, which is being vigilantly pursued by those in authority. It has been suggested that the mysterious personage referred to landed in Liverpool from America, but this so far is no more than a suggestion.

A well-informed correspondent states that he has gleaned the following information from an undeniably authentic source, and from careful and persistent inquiries in various quarters, he is able to relate the news as fact, though for obvious reasons names and addresses are for the present suppressed. A certain member of the Criminal Investigation Department had recently journeyed to Liverpool, and there traced the movements of a man which have proved of a mysterious kind. The height of this person and the description generally are fully ascertained, and among other things he was in possession of a black leather bag. This man suddenly left Liverpool for London, and for some time occupied apartments in a well-known first class hotel in the West End. It is stated that for some reason or another, this person was in the habit of 'slumming'. He would visit the lowest parts of London, and scout the slums of the East End. He suddenly disappeared from the hotel, leaving behind the black leather bag and the contents, and has not returned. He left a small bill unpaid, and ultimately an advertisement appeared in the Times, setting forth the gentleman's name, and drawing attention to the fact that the bag would have been sold under the Innkeepers Act to defray expenses, unless claimed. This was done last month by a well-known auctioneer in London, and the contents, or some of them, are now in the possession of the police, who are thoroughly investigating the affair. Of these, we, of course, cannot more than make mention, but certain documents, wearing apparel, cheque books, prints of an obscene description, letters, etc., and said to form the foundation of a most searching enquiry now on foot, which is being vigilantly pursued by those in authority. It has been suggested that the mysterious personage referred to landed in Liverpool from America, but this so far is no more than a suggestion. The Globe. 9 October 1888.

INNKEEPERS ACT, 41 and 42 Vic., Cap. 38.—
Notice is hereby given, that UNLESS the LUGGAGE LEFT at the CHARING-CROSS HOTEL, West Strand, London, consisting of wearing apparel and personal effects, previous to the 15th September, 1887, is CLAIMED and all charges thereon paid before the 31st May next, in the names undermentioned, the same will be SOLD by Public AUCTION to defray expenses :—G. Hilbert, A. Bayley, M. Lehfeldt, Miss West, S. E. Mibrac, G. Matthew, C. T. Cantillon, F. Desbao, Lake Price, Siger, E. A. R. Verbeek, Captain White, E. Courtois, J. A. Jenkins, A. Harper, L. Young, C. E. Thomas, A. St. Clair, Dr. Young, Skrine, Count de Bnsky, J. Solomons, Captain L. Owen.   By order,   G. S. HAINES, Secretary.
Charing-cross-chambers, Duke-street, Adelphi,
13th April, 1888.

The publication in the Times six months earlier, to which reference was made, listed the bags belonging to one of twenty persons who had left unclaimed luggage in the Charing Cross Hotel, one of whom was 'S.E. Mibrac'. Why all this fuss over a black bag listed as lost property in an article six months earlier, on the 13th April, and how could the instigator of the Globe editorial have linked all this unsubstantiated intrigue to the owner of a black bag in a lost property article? The tale had obviously been contrived and leaked to the press by none other than Michael Maybrick, under the guise of a 'well-informed correspondent'. Liverpool is mentioned twice in the Globe article, as well as America, where Michael's brother James had lived, prior to his return to Liverpool four years earlier in 1884. Appearing only nine days after the double murder in Berner Street and Mitre Square, this was an obtuse attempt to deflect attention to a mystery man, similar in many respects to his brother James. It was certainly much ado about nothing, the article disappeared into obscurity as quickly as it had appeared, and that was the end of the matter, but should Michael even be suspected of involvement in the Whitechapel Murders, the article would be a useful defence, to deflect guilt in the direction of his own brother. Such were the machinations played out in the mind of a man totally devoid of conscience.

The publication in the Times six months earlier, to which reference was made, listed the bags belonging to one of twenty persons who had left unclaimed luggage in the Charing Cross Hotel, one of whom was named 'S.E. Mibrac'. The incriminating contents of the leather bag, as described in the Globe article, would explain why the bag had not been reclaimed, an ongoing source of annoyance to the owner, 'S.E. Mibrac', a pathologically deranged schizophrenic, who would go on to murder two women in Berner Street and Mitre Square. Having already sent two letters to the press claiming responsibility, the murderer was already revelling in his achievements, proud of his kills, and delighting in the stupidity of his pursuers, and the Globe article now provided a further outlet with which to confuse his pursuers.

The Times advertisement of the 18th April 1888 referred to luggage left prior to the 15th September 1887, so occupancy must have been prior to that date, confirming that 'S.E. Mibrac', in reality residing close to Regent's Park, was then in the habit of casually occupying hotel rooms only a couple of miles away, intent on anonymity, well before settling into the lair at St. Jude's Church. Such hotel bases would most definitely not have been used for casual liaisons with the whores of Whitechapel, as Michael Maybrick's inclinations were orientated in an entirely different direction, and the need for privacy in his nefarious activities would have been of paramount importance, unconnected to his home address.

So what evidence was there to link Michael Maybrick with S.E. Mibrac, and hence the articles in the Globe and Liverpool Daily Post, published just after the double murders? Consider the following:

The letters MIBRAC are all in MAYBRICK.

MAYBRICK and S.E. MIBRAC contain the same number of letters.

The letters 'S' and 'E' are specifically separated, rather than included in one word, e.g. MISBRACE or SCIMBARE.

Re-arranging the letters of MIBRAC produces MA*BRIC*, leaving missing letters 'Y' and 'K.'

So how do 'S' and 'E' equate with 'Y' and 'K'? Michael Maybrick was creating, not deciphering, and had countless hours available on tedious long distance train journeys, doodling on notepad after notepad. One of the simplest ways of encoding is a form of Caesar cypher, in which each letter of the alphabet is substituted by the following letter. Hence 'A' equals 'B', 'B' equals 'C', 'C' equals 'D' etc. One move would be too obvious, so the code could be improved, exemplified as follows, below, by progressive forward moves.

1 move	2 moves	3 moves	4 moves	5 moves	6 moves
A=B	A=C	A=D	A=E	A=F	A=G
B=C	B=D	B=E	B=F	B=G	B=H
C=D	C=E	C=F	C=G	C=H	C=I

Six forward moves of 'S' and 'E', produce not only a favourable, but a magical result.

1 move	2 moves	3 moves	4 moves	5 moves	6 moves
S=T	S=U	S=V	S=W	S=X	S=Y
E=F	E=G	E=H	E=I	E= J	E=K

With six forward moves, 'S' and 'E' become 'Y' and 'K', which when added to MIBRAC, produce MAYBRICK.

This was, of course, immaterial to the contents of the Globe article, which served its own nefarious purpose. 'S.E. Mibrac' simply serves to illustrate Michael Maybrick's existing pre-occupation with anagrams and cryptograms before September 1887, well in advance of the outset of the Funny Little Game a year later, when letters would be plucked from the names of innocent women, selected for execution.

JOHN LARDY

On the 19th October, the following article appeared in the Evening News, the contents of which must have severely shaken the imperturbable Michael Maybrick.

A conference took place yesterday afternoon between a young man named John Lardy, of Redman's Row, Mile End, and the head of the detective department at the Old Jewry, which he stated as follows. At 10.30 last night, I was with a friend and a young woman outside the Grave Maurice Tavern opposite the London Hospital, when I noticed a man I had never seen before come across the road, look into each compartment of the tavern and enter the house. He came out again directly, and

The Grave Maurice Tavern

carefully, looked up and down the road, then walked over the road to the front of the hospital, where two women were standing. They were, I believe, loose women. The man said something to them, but I did not hear his words. The women shook their heads and said 'No'. I said to my friend, 'What a funny looking man. I wonder if he is the murderer?' My friend replied, 'Let us follow him.' We said goodnight to our friend, and followed the man. When opposite the Pavilion Theatre, he drew himself up in an instant, and carefully looked around. We believe he saw us, and he disappeared into a doorway. We stopped for a moment or two, and he came out of his hiding place, and went into a shop next door. During the whole time that we saw him, his right hand was in his pocket, apparently clutching something. He bought a paper at the shop, looking up and down the road as he did so, and carefully reading the placards outside the shop window. He afterwards started off towards Aldgate, and we followed him. When he got to the corner of Duke Street (the street leading to Mitre Square) he turned, and seeing that we were following him, re-crossed the road, and walked back to Leman Street, and went down it. When he reached Royal Mint Street, he went into King Street, which is very narrow, and my friend and I ran to the other end of the street, hoping to see him come out there. Just as we got to the other end of King Street, we heard a door close, and we waited to see if the man re-opened it, for we felt sure that he was the man, although we had not seen him go into the house. We waited for 25 minutes, when we saw the same man come out of the house. He came up the street, and we stepped back and allowed him to pass, and he went in the

The Pavilion Theatre.

direction of the Whitechapel Road. He went away, and lost sight of him in the fog, which was then very thick. The

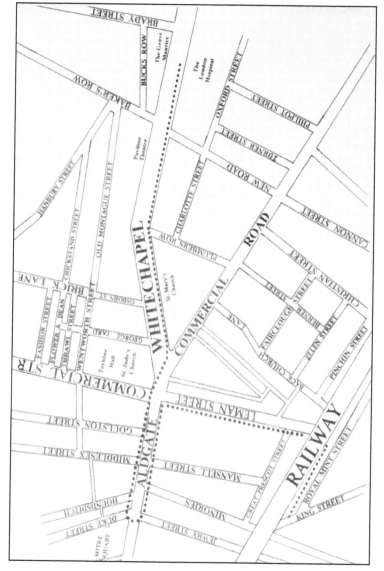

John Lardy's Route

time was just after 12.00. When he re-appeared from the house, we noticed that he was dressed very differently to what he was when we first saw him, the most noticeable thing being his overcoat. At first, he was wearing a sort of short frock-coat, reaching his knees only, but when he came out of the house in King Street he had on a large overcoat, which reached to within three inches off the ground. From what I could see, he appeared to be between forty and fifty years of age, and from five feet eleven inches to six feet tall. A man of five feet eleven inches was placed before Lardy, who said 'My man was a little taller than you.' He wore a low hat with a square crown, but I cannot describe his trousers or boots. He had the appearance of an American. His cheek bones were high and prominent, his face thin, his cheeks sunken, and he had a moustache only, his cheeks and chin being clean shaven. The moustache was, I believe, a false one, for it was all awry, one end pointing upwards, and the other towards the ground. His hair was dark, apparently black and somewhat long. The Central News says: 'It is stated that the man called Lardy attended at the City Police Office in Old Jewry yesterday, but that no importance is attached to his statements.   Evening News. 19 October 1888.

This incident, occurring two days prior to the newspaper report, and four weeks before the murder in Mitre Square, was probably the most important and overlooked piece of evidence in the hunt for Jack the Ripper, but no further action was taken by the police. In the meantime, descriptions of male suspects of all shapes and sizes continued to flood in.

After the Mitre Square Murder, the base in King Street would have been out of the question, and the final part of the game would have to be played out back on home ground, closer to St. Jude's Church. In the meantime, Stephen Adams also had a job to do, with a busy professional schedule of stage performances throughout the Home Counties, North of England, and Scotland, away from his part-time voluntary work, guarding the poor unfortunates of Whitechapel from a lunatic serial killer. A substantial income was rolling into the bank account on a regular basis from musical royalties, including 'They All Love Jack', feeding the ravenous ego with public adulation, bolstering the man's insatiable self-importance and overbearing pomposity. The live performance circuit extended to Manchester, Edinburgh, Glasgow, Dublin, Sheffield, Liverpool, Swansea, Blackpool, Derby, Northampton, Bolton and Leeds, as well as the London venues of Covent Garden and the Theatre Royal, Drury Lane. Train journeys offered both time and opportunity to muse and plan accordingly, and another letter was dispatched, which, whilst undated, is listed on the numerical records of the police files, as having been received on the 23rd October.

I am going to say that I'm not going to rip any more up in Whitechapel but one, and that is one that was kicking up a row outside a public house in Commercial Road a few nights ago. I am going to Poplar and Bromley and Plaistow. Five nice fat in I got. I will give em fossicks. I live in a dust yard my name is (Me yes still ripping em up). You will hear of me tomorrow a good un because it is my birthday.

James Maybrick's 50th birthday was the 24th October 1888, the day after the letter was received, implicating James as the author of the letter. Why would the author be 'living in a dust yard'? In Victorian times, ash from residential and commercial fires would be dumped by residents into pits for collection by workmen, and stored in central dust yards, which were essentially re-cycling centres. The principal residues in the ash, breeze and clinker, were used for the manufacture of bricks, with about ten barges a day leaving the dust yards of the City of London for the brickworks, each carrying 70 tonnes of mixed residue.

154

Michael Maybrick was a top level cryptologist, fifteen years prior to the invention of the crossword puzzle, hence the word 'brick', as in 'Maybrick', living in a dustyard, followed by the incongruously contrived (Me yes), providing the letters M and Y to form 'M-ybrick'. Significantly, the letter claims there was to be only one more victim, as dictated by the Funny Little Game, with the victim frequenting a public house in Commercial Road. Time would soon reveal the mischief behind that little piece of misdirection, away from the intended location, the Britannia public house in Commercial Street.

If we assume that Jack did have a base within the area, circumscribed by his crimes, then various forms of analysis are open to us. One approach, for example, is to assume that the crimes describe a region of activity spreading out from the base. On this assumption the base would be in the middle of our notional circle. But human activity is rarely so symmetrical, and I have found in many studies that the centre of the circle is not the closest estimate to the offender's home, although the home is frequently not far from the geometric centre. In the case of the Whitechapel Murders, this would put the residence somewhere a little north of where Commercial Road meets Whitechapel Road.

Mapping Murder. David Canter

JAMES MAYBRICK

James Maybrick was born in 1838, the second oldest of five boys, although it was acknowledged within the family that when it came to decision making, Michael had always been in charge, effectively assuming the role of head of the household.

FLORENCE AND JAMES MAYBRICK.

In the early days, as Michael pursued his musical career, James endured the daily routine of a broker's clerk in Liverpool, entailing travel to and from London, where, around the year 1860, he met Sarah Ann Robertson, a hair jeweller's assistant. A romance ensued, and whilst there is no documentary evidence of a wedding ceremony, in the 1871 census Sarah is listed as Sarah

Maybrick, married, born in Sunderland, age 33, and living in Bromley Street, Stepney. In the same census, however, James Maybrick is listed as still living in the family home in Mount Pleasant, Liverpool, with his mother, and brothers Thomas and Edwin.

By the time of the next census, ten years later, Sarah had exercised her lady's prerogative by ageing only two years, giving her age as 35, but reverting to her maiden name of Sarah Robertson, born in Sunderland, no occupation. At the time of Sarah's death in 1927, the documentation refers to Sarah Ann Maybrick, otherwise Robertson. Clearly, Sarah was under the Maybrick spell, never wanting to let go of James, and evidently marrying no-one else. James acquiesced in this arrangement, continuing life in Liverpool, conveniently 200 miles away, with regular business trips to London, and the welcoming arms of Sarah.

In 1873, with younger brother Edwin as junior partner, James formed Maybrick and Company, Cotton Merchants, based initially in Liverpool, and soon expanding into the United States, where they established an office in Norfolk, Virginia, on Chesapeake Bay. The business flourished, but a set-back occurred in 1877, when James contracted malaria, for which, of various purported 'cures', the most popular was 'Fowler's Solution', which contained arsenic in manageable proportions. Surprisingly, arsenic was a drug of choice at the time for those seeking the equivalent of a 'legal high', and James Maybrick, a hypochondriac by nature, developed a serious obsession for the poison, which soon developed into a secret addiction.

Over the next few years business prospered, providing a comfortable middle class lifestyle for the two eligible bachelors.

James considered himself a ladies' man, enjoying several relationships whilst in America, but all changed in March 1880, on board the S.S. Baltic in mid-Atlantic en route back to Liverpool, when occurred a pivotal moment in his life. James was introduced to Florence Chandler, 18 years old, travelling to Paris with her mother, Baroness Caroline von Roques, and despite being closer in age to her mother, James was irresistibly attracted to the charismatic blue-eyed belle from Mobile, Alabama, with curvaceous hourglass figure and curly golden locks. Strangely enough, Florence was equally attracted to James, every inch the English gentleman, albeit over twice her age. Only fifteen years had passed since the end of the American Civil War, and Florence's mother, leading by example, being thrice married, ultimately to a German baron, had stressed the importance of courting material wealth and security, rather than fall to the charms of handsome young opportunists on the prowl in Alabama. James could not believe his good luck, and, in July 1881, fourteen months after the whirlwind shipboard romance, before Florie came to her senses, the couple were married at a lavish ceremony in St. James' Church, Piccadilly, London, the city where resided the other Mrs. Maybrick.

Florence was used to being pampered, and James was only too pleased to oblige, indulging his new bride in a protracted honeymoon through France and Italy. No expense was spared on treating Florie to the very finest attire; gowns of silk, chiffon and Chantilly lace, hats adorned with silk flowers and bold ostrich feathers, fur stoles of ermine and mink, and the latest designs in leather boots and shoes. As for jewellery, Florie had her choice of brooches, necklaces, ear-rings, anything, in fact, to bring a smile to the face of James's young bride. Neither was James averse to self-indulgence, ensuring his appearance as a dapper

English gentleman, effusing casual and unspoken wealth, purveyed only by the best tailors of Savile Row and Jermyn Street.

The charade could not last forever, but James had certainly convinced the impressionable young bride that ahead lay the life of luxury of which she had dreamed, whilst sharing aspirations with her fellow fledglings at society balls in Alabama, sophisticated salons in Paris, and finishing school for privileged young ladies in Germany, where Florie had honed her skills in French and German.

Florence had been introduced briefly to brothers Michael and Edwin at the wedding reception, and initial impressions were of the pronounced difference between the two brothers. Michael had the reputation of a jovial baritone singer, the darling of London theatre audiences, but their first encounter had been unusually formal, almost frosty, and the young bride had felt rather unwelcome, a feeling shared by her mother, the Baroness von Roques. Younger brother Edwin, on the other hand, was cheerful, charming, and very good looking. Florence really liked Edwin.

Eight months into the marriage, Florence gave birth to baby James, known affectionately as 'Bobo', and the pair accompanied James across the Atlantic, settling down to married life in Virginia, where James continued his secret addiction. In 1884, it became clear that the American side of the business was in decline, due to a slump in the cotton market, and it was resolved that Edwin would remain in Virginia to maintain the American contact, whilst James and family would return to Liverpool, renting a house from his 'friend' Mrs. Matilda Briggs, who, as one of three Janion sisters, had fluttered her eyelashes at James years prior to her marriage in 1871 to wealthy local man of property, Horace Briggs. Needless to say, on their return to Liverpool, Jim was still in favour with Matty, and always would be, instanced by the offer of renting her house, now in her sole ownership, following a deed of separation from her husband. Matilda obligingly moved into her mother's residence nearby, together with her mother and children, all soon becoming well acquainted with the Maybrick family.

In 1888, the Maybricks moved to a rented mansion, Battlecrease House, located in Aigburth, a prestigious residential area on the outskirts of Liverpool, where appearances were considered essential, but whilst appearing happily ensconced in their new residence, all was not well within the marriage.   Evidently Florence suspected James of infidelity, and reacted by flirting with brother Edwin, whilst James continued to gulp his favourite Fowler's Solution, supplemented by occasional doses of arsenic, as and when available.

During the course of the Whitechapel murders, James and Michael must have talked about Jack the Ripper, as such was the talk in every township in the land, and the question has to be asked whether James secretly harboured the idea that his brother Michael was a candidate for the title.   James knew his brother's idiosyncrasies better than anyone, was well versed in his weird mood swings, and had often experienced his propensity for strange behaviour.   Had the thought also occurred to Florence, and had James mentioned her suspicions whilst in conversation with Michael?   Very possibly, if not likely.   Florence, who had found Michael cold and unfriendly, could be very outspoken after her second glass of sherry, and more so Champagne.   Gossip spreads like wildfire, and Florence could be potentially dangerous, mixing in Liverpool social circles as she did on occasions.   Now that James had raised the subject, he too, could prove another weak link, which Michael could well do without. The threat of dangling by the neck on the end of a rope tends to concentrate the mind, and that of a psychopathic serial killer has no empathy, no conscience, absolutely no sense of right or wrong. James was already well on the road to self-destruction through his drug habit, and the devious plan to involve James ripened further in the Machiavellian mind of Michael Maybrick.

Whilst on business trips to London, James would meet up with Michael, regularly updating him with ongoing events in his life, as the result of which Michael would have known every detail of their marital problems, holding them both in contempt, James for his stupidity in falling for Florence, and Florence for being no more than a strumpet and, in his eyes, a whore.   All was logged into Michael's tormented delusional mindset, for future reference, if need be.   Perhaps he made notes, lest one day he would write a diary, featuring his brother.   Just in case.

EMILY MARSH

Michael Maybrick thrived on fame and adulation, composer of best-selling ballads as Stephen Adams, adored by theatrical audiences as Mr. Michael Maybrick, and basking in notoriety as the most wanted man in the land as the Whitechapel Murderer. Driven by a sense of narcissistic invincibility to leave mischievous clues, some understood only by Freemasons, he was on a personal high, in a world of his own, semi-divine in the shadowy lair of St. Jude's Church, savouring the gradual fulfilment of his Funny Little Game. Luck had been his saviour. Liz Stride had seen him flash the knife, and hence had to die, but two others had also seen him holding the weapon, the assailant, who had been detained, and the Hungarian Schwartz, who had recounted the tale to the newspapers, alongside Maybrick's description, as the mysterious tall man.

The police have arrested one man answering the description the Hungarian furnishes. The prisoner has not been charged, but is being held for enquiries to be made. The Star. 1 October 1888.

Michael Maybrick knew something wasn't quite right. Both Schwartz and the assailant would have already provided a damning description of him, without disguise, yet there had been no press release from the police. Schwartz had told the Star reporter that, as viewed by poor street lighting, the 'second man' was aged about 35 years old, around five feet eleven inches tall, with fresh complexion, light brown hair, and brown moustache. Maybrick would have appreciated this flattering description, knocking 12 years off his age, but he was in prime condition, and this misconception was a regular occurrence.

Michael Maybrick puts his whole strength and soul into everything he does. He possesses the muscle and brawn of an

ideal Life Guardsman, and his passion for every form of outdoor
pursuit has enabled him to retain the full vigour of youth much
longer than the rest of his contemporaries.

New York World. 15 January 1891.

It was however, a disconcertingly close description, and he could
be in serious trouble, particularly in an area where the average
male height was five feet five inches, and complexions were in
the main dark or 'foreign'. Yet, quite incredibly, ten days after
the double murder, Michael Maybrick would once again chance
his luck in Whitechapel, this time in broad daylight, sporting a
false beard and clerical attire, conveniently borrowed from the
robing room at St. Jude's Church, little realising that this
clandestine venture would be reported in the press.

At the inquest of Catherine Eddowes, or 'Mary Ann Kelly,' the
Coroner had confirmed the right kidney had been cut out and
taken away by the killer. The following article was published in
the Daily Telegraph, three weeks after the disappearance of the
kidney, and the day after the John Lardy report in the press.

A statement that apparently gives a clue to the sender of the
strange package received by Mr. Lusk was made last night by
Miss Emily Marsh, whose father carries on business in the leather
trade at 218 Jubilee Street, Mile End Road. In Mr. Marsh's
absence Miss Marsh was in the front shop, shortly after one
o'clock on Monday last, when a stranger dressed in clerical
costume entered, and, referring to the reward in the window,
asked for the address of Mr. Lusk, described therein as the
President of the Vigilance Committee. Miss Marsh at once
referred the man to Mr. Aarons, the Treasurer of the Committee,
who resides at the corner of Jubilee Street and Mile End Road, a
distance of thirty yards. The man, however, said he did not wish
to go there, and Miss Marsh then produced a newspaper in which
Mr. Lusk's address was given in Alderney Road, no number being

mentioned. She requested the stranger to read the address, but he declined, saying, 'Read it out', and proceeded to write something in his copy book, keeping his head down meanwhile. He subsequently left the shop, after thanking the young lady for the information, but not before Miss Marsh, alarmed by the man's appearance, had sent the shop boy, John Cormack, to see that all was right. This lad, as well as Miss Marsh, gave a full description of the man, whilst Mr. Marsh, who happened to come along at the time, also encountered him on the pavement outside

The stranger is described as a man of some forty five years of age, fully six feet tall in height, and slimly built. He wore a soft felt black hat, drawn over his forehead, a stand-up collar, and a very long black single-breasted overcoat, with Prussian or clerical collar partly turned up. His face was of a sallow type, and he had a dark beard and moustache. The man spoke with what was taken as an Irish accent. No importance was attached to the incident until Miss Marsh read of the receipt by Mr. Lusk of a strange parcel, and it then occurred to her that the stranger might have been the person who had despatched it. This inquiry was made at one o'clock on Monday afternoon, and Mr. Lusk received the package at eight pm the next day. The address of the package curiously gives no number in Alderney Road, a piece of information which Miss Marsh could not supply. It appears that on leaving the shop, the man went right by Mr. Aaron's house, but did not call. Mr. Lusk states that no person answering the description had called on him, nor does he know anyone like the man in question. Daily Telegraph. 20 October 1888.

The description of the man bears an uncanny resemblance to the man followed two days earlier by John Lardy. Yet, once again, the 'tall man' link seems to have been overlooked by the police, unless, of course, Inspector Abberline had his own theories. In the post the following day, George Lusk, President of the newly formed Whitechapel Vigilance Committee, received a parcel containing half a human kidney, addressed to his home in

Alderney Road, but with no house number, conforming exactly to Emily Marsh's version of events. Enclosed in the parcel was a letter deliberately mis-spelled, and headed 'From Hell'.

Mr. Lusk, From Hell

Sor, I send you half the kidne I took from one women prasarved it for you tother piece I fried and ate it was very nise. I may send you the bloody knif that took it out if you only wate a whil longer signed Catch me when you can Mishter Lusk.

The letter is a crude attempt at disguised handwriting 'in an Irish accent', a big mistake by the theatrical Mr. Michael Maybrick, as Irishmen don't write in an Irish accent. The letter must have been penned by the fake clergyman, providing a direct link to the kidney, and thus the killer. Emily was not a child, but was 18 years old, as confirmed in the National Census, and was chosen not at random, but for a more ominous reason. Emily Marsh possessed not only the deadly 'MA' virus in her name, but a highly significant 'Em Ma' which may well have triggered the Emma reaction in Maybrick's twisted mindset. Was it just his appearance that upset Emily, or was it the weird behaviour of a man possessed of an overwhelming urge to hurt her, but in the wrong place to do so? The trigger reaction had been predictably spontaneous given the girl's name, and with unpredictable consequences, but once the shop boy appeared, self-preservation was of paramount importance, and a speedy exit was called for, leaving Emily sufficiently traumatised as to immediately alert the boy and then her father, hardly a normal reaction to simply odd behaviour. Emily had been very frightened indeed. It was a close call. An arrest at the Marsh's shop would have closed the case, had the 'priest' been apprehended and stripped of his disguise, but it didn't happen, and the parcel was duly posted. The message was clear, 'Catch me when you can, but you never will, because I am so very, very clever!', a personal riposte to Brother George Lusk of Doric Lodge No.933, for daring to consider himself capable of catching Brother Michael Maybrick. No such taunts, however, were directed towards Inspector Frederick Abberline of Scotland Yard, who had taken very seriously the description of the six foot man with the dark beard. On the contrary, a measure of respect is shown in the Maybrick Diary.

Oh Mr. Abberline, he is a clever little man,
He keeps back all he can,
For do I not know better, indeed I do,
Did I leave him a very good clue.
Nothing is mentioned, of this I am sure,
Ask clever Abberline, could tell you more.

The Diary of Jack the Ripper.

Throughout the nineteenth century, and for a long time afterwards, the minimum height requirement for a police officer was 5 feet 10 inches. Inspector Frederick Abberline, at half an inch less, had only just scraped in, but he was still above the height of the average male in Whitechapel. However, only a taller man would have referred to him as a clever 'little' man. Michael Maybrick was 6 feet one inch tall.

Four weeks earlier, Inspector Abberline had been on vigil at the London Hospital, waiting to interview Margaret Millous, seriously attacked and injured hours before the murder of Mary Ann Nichols. No details had been released to the British Press, but Margaret's rescuer had provided information to the American press to the effect that the assailant was a tall man with a black beard, information which was locked inside Inspector Abberline's head. Whilst the press was pursuing five feet four inch Leather Apron lookalikes, or five feet eight inch blonde sailors, Inspector

Abberline was quietly pursuing his own agenda, involving a suspect six feet tall, with light brown hair, sallow complexion, a reddy brown moustache, and false black beard when appropriate. An officer worthy of the rank of Inspector in Scotland Yard would have been busy narrowing the search to persons around that height, legitimately on the street in the hours after midnight, and top of the list would have been policemen, with steps being taken to check the records. Next in line should have been members of the Vigilance Associations, 'Just a few routine questions, sir, which we're addressing to all members of the Vigilance Associations.' Whether or not such enquiries were instigated will never be known, but Michael Maybrick certainly behaved differently during and after the month of October. St. Jude's Church would have been avoided for a while, and although on tour in provincial theatres for a great deal of the time, the very fact that Abberline was sniffing around was unnerving, even to the imperturbable Michael Maybrick.

Maybrick had soon become attached to the new sobriquet of Jack the Ripper, even taking exception to two small articles published in the Liverpool Echo on the 9th October, the first of which claimed that Jack the Ripper had written to the Dublin authorities advising of his intention to visit Dublin that

> connection with the Whitechapel murder. The Dublin police authorities have received a letter purporting to be from "Jack the Ripper," stating that he intends visiting Dublin this week.
>
> ### "JACK THE RIPPER" AT AN IRISH COURSING MATCH.
>
> [SPECIAL TELEGRAM.]
> Yesterday, at Dearham, near Maryport, during a rabbit coursing match, a dog named Jack the Ripper went down in the first round. When it was announced that one of the coursing dogs was named after the alleged Whitechapel murderer the spectators indulged in derisive yells, and when it was defeated they cheered lustily.

> A LIVERPOOL FANATIC.
> The subjoined communication was addressed to the Liverpool Echo office yesterday on an ordinary postcard :—
>
> Stafford-street.
> Dear Sir,—I beg to state that the letters published in yours of yesterday are lies. It is somebody gulling the public. I am the Whitechapel purger. On 13th, at 3 p.m., will be on Stage, as am going to New York. But will have some business before I go.—Yours truly,
> Jack the Ripper. DIEGO LAURENZ.
> (Genuine.)

167

week. The next article referred to a humorous incident regarding an Irish dog named Jack the Ripper, which may have accounted for the mischievous response to both articles, in a postcard addressed to the editor of the Liverpool Echo, printed the following day. To have seen the articles in the Liverpool Echo, and have responded so quickly, the reader must have been in Maybrick's home town of Liverpool, the main ferry link to Dublin. Unfortunately, the postcard was not retained, and only the newspaper article remains.

Dear Sir,   *Stafford Street.*

I beg to state that the letters published in yours of yesterday, are lies. It is somebody gulling the public. I am the Whitechapel purger. On 13th October at 3 pm will be on Stage, as I am going to New York. But will have some business before I go.
Yours truly Diego Laurenz. Jack the Ripper. (Genuine).

Addressed to the editor of the Liverpool Echo, the subliminal inference is that the content refers to a ship sailing from Liverpool landing stage on the 13th October, bound for New York. Not so. Michael Maybrick is playing mind games, 'gulling the public'. The postcard makes no reference whatsoever to Liverpool, only 'on stage' and 'New York'. A clever piece of misdirection. As confirmed in the Cunard

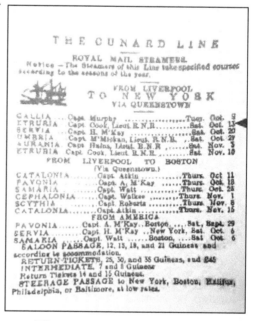

168

Line billboards, the S.S. Etruria was indeed due to sail from Liverpool to New York on the 13th October. However, also on that day the S.S. Umbria was 'on stage' in 'New York', as per the carefully worded postcard, under the command of Captain William McMickan, whose name contains five of the eight letters in Maybrick, the Whitechapel purger.

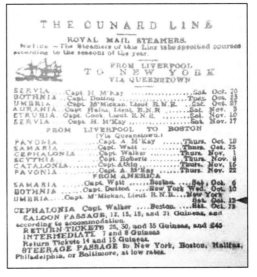

Why the incongruous reference to Stafford Street? Contemporary Liverpool street maps confirm that Stafford Street runs between London Road and Islington, and hence into Soho Street. London, Islington, Soho, Whitechapel. Another source of personal amusement which no-one else would understand.

The name 'Diego Laurenz', written next to 'Jack the Ripper', is the most obvious of the cryptic clues in the postcard. Diego is Spanish for James, whilst Laurenz bears an almost identical phonetic resonance to James's wife Florence, both living in Liverpool, in a house rented from family friend Matilda Briggs, living nearby with her mother Domatila Rodriguez Janion, daughter of the Chilean Consul to Hawaii. Both were regular visitors to the Maybrick household, and Domatila's native language was Spanish, raising the real likelihood that James would indeed have been referred to as 'Diego'. In 1886, when

Florence gave birth to their second child, Gladys Evelyn, Domatila was invited to be the infant's godmother.

The latent inference within the postcard is James, alias the signatory Diego, is Jack the Ripper. Elder brother James was not as tall as Michael, but was well above average height, with fair hair and brown moustache. He also visited London on occasions. No harm would come of this little play on words, simply a strange postcard which no one would ever interpret, no malice intended. Michael was well aware this little snippet would be logged on police files, only to be brought out into play in the event of dire necessity, which surely would never happen, but nothing lost, and privately so very amusing. James need never know of his potential involvement in this twisted contingency scheme, held in reserve lest the finger of suspicion began to show movement in Michael's direction. The stark reality, however, was that for such a contingency plan to succeed, James would have to be dead.

RESIGNATION

Pressure to resign had been mounting on Sir Charles Warren since his heavy-handed mismanagement of the Trafalgar Square protest a year earlier. A military man through and through, he had introduced army drill and discipline into the Metropolitan Police, resulting in dissent and resentment within the ranks. An unhappy police force is an inefficient police force, and, as the Whitechapel murders continued unabated and undetected, the press soon became involved.

The Whitechapel mystery is a mystery still. That is the terrible fact that the Government and Sir Charles Warren have to consider this morning. We are hourly receiving fresh evidence of the utter inadequacy and unskilfulness of the police. Out of the 2,600 men who are responsible at night for the safety of the inhabitants of London, not a tenth, not a twentieth, are capable of efficient detective work. To add to the list of clumsy follies which have made Sir Charles Warren's name stink in the nostrils of the people of London, the Chief Commissioner has lately transferred the whole of the East End detectives to the West, and moved the West End men to the East. That is to say, he has deprived the people of Whitechapel of the one guarantee they had for reposing confidence in their ordinary guardian. Whitechapel, then, is particularly defenceless. The Star. 10 September 1888.

It looks very much as if the police have entirely lost the scent of the Whitechapel murderer, if, indeed, they ever found it. Charles Warren ought to go. Of course, he, and not Mr. Matthews, is really to blame. A feeble, forcible red tapist, with the mind of a dancing master and the statesmanship of an apprentice's clerk, like Mr. Matthews, is, of course, unsuitable for his position, but with a just and really strong man in Scotland Yard, Mr. Matthews could have done little harm. It is Sir Charles Warren who has militarised the force when he ought to have spiritualised, and

171

trained it. Less drill and more brains, less of 'Prepare to meet the cavalry', and more of 'Prepare to catch criminals', is what is wanted in our police. The Star. 13 September. 1888.

The Chief Commissioner even declared that he could have solved the murder himself, had sufficient time been available. Just where did his priorities lie? Evidently out of the firing line, and as far from Whitechapel as possible, but also believing in the need to contain the search for the killer within a small band of Masonic brothers, within the Metropolitan Police.

I am convinced that the Whitechapel murder case is one that can be successfully grappled with, if it is systematically taken in hand. I go so far as to say that I could myself unravel the mystery, provided I could spare the time, and give individual attention. I feel therefore the utmost importance to be attached to putting the whole Central Office work in this case in the hands of one man, who will have nothing else to concern himself with. I give him the whole responsibility.
Sir Charles Warren. Memo to Home Office. 15 September 1888.

On the 15th September 1888, Brother Sir Charles Warren dictated an in-house police memorandum, delegating all matters relating to the Whitechapel Murders to Detective Inspector Brother Donald Swanson, Lodge of St. Peter's No.284. The memorandum was initialled by the Chief Constable, Brother Adolphus Frederick Williamson, Lodge of Fortitude and Old Cumberland No.12. Such is the art of delegation. If, however, Sir Charles Warren thought for a fleeting moment that delegation to Brother Swanson would take the weight of the Whitechapel murders off his own shoulders, he was very much mistaken. The other party immediately involved in the Whitechapel atrocities at a high level was Inspector Frederick Abberline, who was not a Freemason, which perhaps accounted for his singular reluctance to share information. Every policeman had his eye on

172

promotional prospects within the force, and catching the Whitechapel Murderer would be Inspector Abberline's personal passport to success He had his own thoughts on the matter, which he intended to keep to himself. In the meantime, public resentment against Sir Charles Warren was mounting, and protest rallies were organised in various parts of London.

At three o'clock yesterday afternoon, a meeting of nearly one thousand persons took place in Victoria Park. A resolution was unanimously passed that it was high time both the Home Secretary and Sir Charles Warren should resign, and make way for some officers who would leave no stone unturned for the purpose of bringing the murderer to justice. On Mile End waste during the day, four meetings of the same kind were held and similar resolutions passed. Pall Mall Gazette. 1 October 1888.

Immediately following the double murder on the 30th September, Sir Charles Warren had commissioned the trial of bloodhounds in Hyde Park, which proved successful, including one in which Warren himself led the chase as the victim. This, at last, promised a definite means with which to catch the Whitechapel Murderer, but the press rightly queried why these measures had not been adopted earlier, before more lives had been lost.

Sir Charles Warren has at length approved the use of bloodhounds for the detection of the East End Murderer. Here were murders taking place under circumstances which pointed to bloodhounds as ideal detectives. In each case the streets were unoccupied, the scent was clear. Dogs may have led straight away to the murderer's retreat, and he would have been caught like a rat in a hole. Why was this not done after the third murder. Or the fourth? The whole thing is simply a monstrous instance of the utter incapacity which characterises Scotland Yard and its distinguished head. The Star. 10 October 1888.

Warren ordered that should another murder occur, the victim was not to be touched, pending the arrival of the bloodhounds. The successful bloodhounds, Barnaby and Bourgho, were offered for sale to the Metropolitan Police, but the owner of the bloodhounds later confirmed that no response had been received to the offer, and the hounds were never engaged in the manhunt. The question has to be asked, was Bro. Sir Charles Warren fearful that the murderer, if sniffed out by the bloodhounds, would be revealed as a Freemason before he had the chance to discover the perpetrator and deal with the matter discreetly. A few days after the double murders, news broke of Sir Charles Warren's erasure of the writing on the wall at Goulston Street.

The case against the Chief Commissioner is overwhelming. In the case of the murder in Mitre Square, the murderer did leave behind him a clue of simply incalculable importance. Yet it has been destroyed, and destroyed by the direct act of Sir Charles Warren himself. If we had been called upon to imagine what would afford the public an exact measure of Sir Charles Warren's utter incapacity for the work he has on hand, we could not have conceived anything more conclusive than this

Pall Mall Gazette. 12 October 1888.

Throughout the month of October, friction continued within the higher echelons of the Metropolitan Police and the Home Office. The Home Secretary and Sir Charles Warren had never really seen eye to eye over most matters; politicians and soldiers rarely agree, and there was a singular lack of trust between the two. The press smelled blood, and took up the chase, increasing pressure on Warren to resign, as a consequence of which, on the 12th November 1888, the Home Secretary, Henry Matthews, made an announcement in the House of Commons, in response to a question on Sir Charles Warren's performance as Commissioner of the Metropolitan Police.

With regard to the question of the Hon. Member for Cambourne, I have to say that the Chief Commissioner did, on the 8th November, tender his resignation to Her Majesty's Government, and that resignation has been accepted. (Loud cheers).

The press were hot on his heels.

Charles Warren may now be reconciled to his bloodhounds. These animals, it will be remembered, mysteriously disappeared, and there is no doubt that, finding they could not get on with the Chief Commissioner, they too had resigned.

The Star. 13 November 1888.

Fun Magazine. 19 September 1888.

ADIEU MARIE

The Funny Little Game was still incomplete, and the final act had to be played out, whatever the risk. Five weeks had passed since the last murders, and police patrols had been stepped up, so the final event would have to be much closer to St. Jude's, minimising the risk of detection. Another tall man sighting would tip the balance towards his capture, albeit Her Majesty's constabulary hadn't performed too well so far. The victim, of course, had to fulfil the necessary 'MA' requirement, and include the letter 'K' in her name, which could have been a tall order, but immediately after the Mary Ann Kelly saga, another Mary Kelly made it known that she was definitely still alive and well, and in

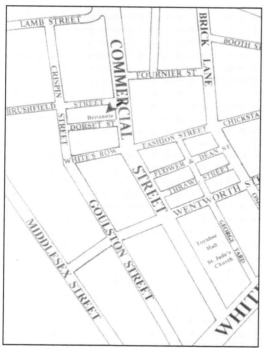

doing so signed her own death warrant. Marie Jeanette Kelly, known locally as Mary Jane Kelly, fulfilled all the requirements for completion of the Funny Little Game, and lived surprisingly close to Toynbee Hall at 13, Miller's Court, Dorset Street, the same street where earlier victim Annie Chapman had lived, prior to her demise. Significantly, at the time of the murders, all the Ripper victims lived within a very short walking distance of the Toynbee Hall exit in Wentworth Street.

Emma Smith	18 George Street
Martha Tabram	19 George Street
Mary Ann Nichols	18 Thrawl Street
Annie Chapman	35 Dorset Street
Liz Stride	32 Flower & Dean Street
Catherine Eddowes	55 Flower & Dean Street
Mary Jane Kelly	13 Miller's Court, Dorset Street

George Street is the narrow lane between Wentworth Street and Fashion Street, passing through Thrawl Street, and Flower and Dean Street. This was an area undoubtedly patrolled by the Vigilance Association, increasing the likelihood of Michael Maybrick having encountered his potential victims on a regular basis, bolstering his credibility as a safe confidant, yet disastrous when resulting in 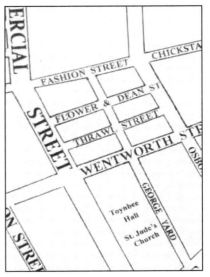 recognition by Liz Stride, whilst on route to Mitre Square. Such was the notoriety of this locality that it prompted an interesting letter to The Times,

Sir,

Let an experiment be made in Dorset Street, Flower and Dean Street, and Thrawl Street, places made notorious in connection with the recent Whitechapel Murders. In these streets, literally

177

within a stone's throw of Toynbee Hall and the Rev. Barnett's Vicarage, are whole rows of so called 'registered' lodging houses, each of which is practically a brothel and a focus for crime. The police authorities uniformly refuse to prosecute the owners of such places as keepers of disorderly houses, and they always throw the odious duty of prosecution on the neighbours who may feel aggrieved. The Times. 29 September 1888.

One neighbour, residing occasionally and unofficially in St. Jude's Church, next door to the Rev. Barnett's Vicarage, felt particularly aggrieved by the local whores, and intended to do something about it. Timing would be crucial to success. There was an even stronger police presence in Whitechapel than at the time of the double murder, but Michael Maybrick had been doing his homework, with meticulous attention to detail. The 9th November was the day of the Lord Mayor's Parade, when all available police would be stationed along the parade route in the city centre, well away from Whitechapel. As a further precaution, the final act of retribution would not be late at night, but early in the morning, indoors, and in the hours of daylight.

The evening of the 8th November was the occasion of the Annual Installation meeting of Charles Warren's Quatuor Coronati Lodge, so what a splendid anniversary present for Brother Charles Warren. Even better, the 9th November was the birthday of Brother HRH Prince Edward, Grand Master of the United Grand Lodge of England, so this would also be a fine birthday present for his fellow member of the Savage Club. What an achievement for the great Michael Maybrick to steal the newspaper headlines from the Lord Mayor's parade, and what a grand finale for the Funny Little Game.

In the days prior to the event, the vigilante had made it his business to encounter and develop a casual acquaintance with

Mary Jane Kelly, also known as 'Fair Emma'. Nothing too obvious, but as close to flattery and flirtation as could be acted by an emotionless psychopathic misogynist.

Another terrible murder, accompanied by hideous mutilation and dismemberment, has spread new panic amongst the populace of East London. It differs indeed from its predecessors in the fact that it has been committed within doors, instead of in the open street, or in a back yard. This, however, would only indicate that the murderer had learned the unusual lesson of caution with success.   Daily Telegraph. 10 November 1888.

13 Miller's Court, Dorset Street.

Success indeed. The mission had gone to plan, and the assassin had disappeared, not into the night, but into broad daylight. At 10.45 am, rent collector Thomas Bowyer called at 13 Miller's Court, Dorset Street, and looked through the window.

The body of the woman, perfectly nude, was stretched out on the little bed, the clothes on which were saturated in blood. The unfortunate woman had been cut and hacked by the assassin's knife in a manner which was revolting beyond all description. The fiendish assailant had exercised an infernal ingenuity in despoiling the corpse of its human semblance. Both ears and nose had been cut off, and the flesh of the cheeks and forehead peeled off, the breasts were cut away, evidently with a sharp knife, and placed on the table near the bed. The abdomen had been ripped open and disembowelled, portions of the entrails lying about the bed, the liver being placed between the legs. Both thighs had been denuded of flesh, laying bare the bones and the excised portions laid on the table. Some of the internal parts of the body had been taken away, while, in addition, one arm was almost severed from the trunk.

Daily News. 10 November 1888.

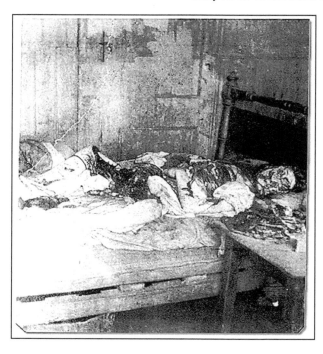

The police were immediately summoned, but when Inspector Abberline arrived at 11.30 am, he was advised by his colleague, Inspector Beck, not to enter as the illusory bloodhounds were on their way. On the recommendation of Dr. Bagster Phillips, the police officers refrained from entering the building until the arrival of Superintendent Thomas Arnold at 1.30 pm, when it was confirmed that there would be no bloodhounds, and the door was broken open, with the butchered body parts of Marie Jeanette Kelly revealed for all to see. Next on the scene were Dr. Thomas Bond, Police Surgeon to the Metropolitan Police, and Dr. Gordon Brown, City Police Surgeon and fellow associate of Michael Maybrick in the Savage Club. The door was closed, and the grisly autopsy commenced. Dr. Bond, who carried out the post-mortem examination, would later write,

The murderer must have been a man of physical strength, and of great coolness and daring. There is no evidence that he had an accomplice. He must, in my opinion, be a man subject to periodical attacks of homicidal and erotic mania. The character of the mutilations indicate that the man may be in a condition sexually that may be called satyriasis. It is, of course, possible that the homicidal impulse may have developed from a revengeful or brooding condition of the mind, or that religious mania may have been the original disease..... The murderer in external appearance is quite likely to be a quiet inoffensive man, probably middle-aged and neatly and respectably dressed. I think he must be in the habit of wearing a cloak or an overcoat, or he could have hardly have escaped notice in the streets, if blood on his hands or clothes were visible. Assuming the murderer to be such a person as I have described he would probably be solitary and eccentric in his habits. He is possibly living amongst respectable persons who have some knowledge of his character and habits, and who have grounds for suspicion that he is not quite right in his mind at times.

Dr. Thomas Bond.

Respectable persons like his brother and sister-in-law, who were now next in line for elimination. Four days later, this article appeared in the Daily Telegraph,

Throughout Saturday and yesterday, the crowd that gathered in Miller's Court was not large, and all night evangelistic services were held in the lodging houses by small bands of men and women. At St. Jude's Church there is a worship hour from 8.30 to 9.30, after the ordinary service. In Toynbee Hall close by, a company of intelligent looking men listened to a discussion, led by Mr. Cunningham, in 'Pleasure and Pain and the Basis of Ethical Systems.' Daily Telegraph. 12 November. 1888.

The poignancy would not have been lost on Michael Maybrick. Perhaps he even attended the meeting, a legitimate excuse to remain in Whitechapel and savour the aftermath of his venture, rather than return to the cloying silence of Regents Park.

Meanwhile, in a different world one hundred miles further north, HRH Prince Edward was celebrating his birthday, totally oblivious to the momentous events in Whitechapel.

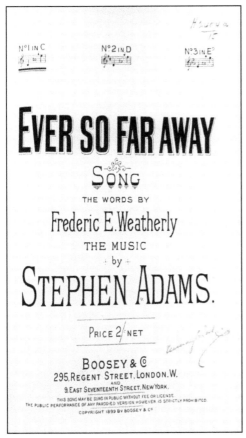

Sandringham. November 9. The Prince of Wales celebrates the 47th anniversary of his birth at his Norfolk seat today in the usual manner. Their Royal Highnesses are entertaining the Duc D'Aumale, and a number of friends. This morning the Prince of Wales, Prince Albert Victor, the Duc D'Aumale, Count Karolyn, the Marquis of Lansdowne, Count Gleichen, Prince Louis Esterhazy, Lord Rowton, Baron Ferdinand Rothschild, and other gentlemen. have shot through the Woodcock Wood. The Princess and the ladies of the party joined the royal sportsmen in the afternoon.

Daily News. 10 November 1888.

ASHES IN THE FIREPLACE

The inquest on Mary Jane Kelly, held on the 12th November, was, at the very least, irregular. Whilst the murder had occurred in the Whitechapel area, the inquest was held at Shoreditch, under Coroner Roderick Macdonald, instead of in the Whitechapel area, under Coroner Wynne Baxter. Once the inquest had been convened, one of the jurymen raised the following objection.

Juryman: *I do not see why we should have this inquest thrown on our shoulders, when the murder did not happen in our district, but in Whitechapel.*
Coroners Officer: It did not happen in Whitechapel.
Juryman: *It is an indisputable fact that Miller's Court, Dorset Street, is most definitely in Whitechapel.*
Coroners Officer: Do you think we do not know what we are doing here, and that we do not know our own district?
Juryman: *I come from Whitechapel, and Mr. Baxter is my Coroner.*
Coroner: *Jurisdiction lies where the body lies, not where it was found, if there is any doubt as to the district where the body was found.*
Juryman: *There was no doubt as to the district where the body was found. It was found in Dorset Street, Whitechapel.*

The Coroner then addressed the reporters, saying a great fuss had been made in some newspapers about the jurisdiction of the Coroner, and who should hold the inquest. He had received no communication from Dr. Baxter upon the subject, the body was in his locality, it had been taken to his mortuary, and there was an end to it. The jurisdiction was where the body lay. There is no doubt, however, that the inquest should have been held in Whitechapel, where the murder had been carried out, and under the jurisdiction of Coroner Baxter. At the previous inquest, Liz Stride's body had rested in St. George's Mortuary, East Stepney, well outside Whitechapel, yet Wynne Baxter, quite rightly, had conducted the inquest in Berner Street, Whitechapel, where the murder had been committed, not where the body lay, contrary to the hollow argument promulgated by Coroner Macdonald. Furthermore, the inquests of earlier victims Annie Chapman, Mary Ann Nichols and Liz Stride had been carried out under Coroner Wynne Baxter, familiar with the modus operandi of the murderer, so why was the logical continuity not maintained in respect of Mary Jane Kelly's inquest under the same Coroner, and in the correct district? Was pressure being exerted by the Establishment to prejudice the direction of the inquest? Was Baxter reluctant to become involved in the Mary Jane Kelly inquest, and did he willingly acquiesce in the case being conducted by Coroner Macdonald?

Abberline may well have discussed with Coroner Baxter the fact that the police were seeking a tall man in connection with the Whitechapel Murders. Had he confided in Wynne Baxter even further, to the effect that perhaps Michael Maybrick ticked all the boxes? Abberline would have been unaware that Brother Wynne Edwin Baxter, Past Master of Burlington Lodge No.98, was a close Masonic friend of Brother Michael Maybrick. Did Abberline's disclosure, with or without foundation, provide further reason for Brother Wynne Baxter to concede the proceedings to Coroner Macdonald? Brother Baxter would have been rightly concerned at Abberline's suspicions, and may have considered having a quiet word with Brother Maybrick on the occasion their paths crossed. Inspector Abberline was totally unaware of the strength of the 'Mystic Tie', which united the Brotherhood of Freemasonry.

As the inquest proceeded, two witnesses were called who claimed to have seen Mary Jane Kelly in the company of a man. Mary Ann Cox, a 'lady of the night', and fellow resident of Miller's Court, testified,

Cox: I last saw her alive at a quarter to twelve, very intoxicated.
Coroner: Was anybody with her?
Cox: A short, stout man, shabbily dressed. He had on a longish coat, very shabby, and carried a pint of ale in his hand.
Coroner: Did you see them go into her room?
Cox: Yes. I said 'Goodnight Mary', and she turned around and banged the door.
Coroner: Did she say anything?
Cox: She said, 'Goodnight, I am going to have a song.' As I went in she was singing 'A violet I plucked from my mother's grave.' I remained a quarter of an hour in my room and went out. Deceased was still singing at one o' clock when I returned. I remained in the room for a minute to warm my hands as it was raining, and went out again. She was singing still, and I returned to my room at 3 o'clock. The light was then out, and there was no noise.
Coroner: What had Mary Jane on?
Cox: She had no hat: a red pelerine and a shabby skirt.

Next to testify was Caroline Maxwell, the wife of a lodging house deputy in Miller's Court, who confirmed that not only had she seen Mary Jane alive and well between eight and nine o'clock the following morning, but had spoken with her.

Coroner: You must be very careful about your evidence, because it is different to other peoples. You say you saw her standing in the corner of the entry to the court?
Maxwell: Yes, on Friday from eight to half-past eight. I fix the time by my husband's finishing work. When I came out of the lodging house, she was opposite.

Coroner: Did you speak to her?

Maxwell: Yes. It was an unusual thing to see her up. She was a young woman who never associated with anyone. I spoke across the street. 'What Mary, brings you up early?' She said, 'Oh, Carrie, I do feel so bad.'

Coroner: What did she say?

Maxwell: She said, 'I've had a glass of beer, and I've brought it up again,' and it was in the road. I imagine she had been in the Britannia beer shop at the corner of the street. I left her, saying I could pity her feelings. I went to Bishopsgate Street to get my husband's breakfast. Returning, I saw her outside the Britannia public house talking to a man.

Coroner: This would be at what time?

Maxwell: Between eight and nine o'clock. I was absent about half an hour. It was about a quarter to nine.

Coroner: What description can you give of this man?

Maxwell: I could not give you any, as they were some distance.

Insp. Abberline: The distance is about sixteen yards,

Maxwell: I am sure it was the deceased. I am willing to swear it.

Coroner: Was he a tall man?

Maxwell: No, he was a little taller than me, and stout.

Insp. Abberline: On consideration, I should say the distance was twenty-five yards.

To ask a leading question such as 'Was he a tall man?' is contrary to accepted procedure, the correct phraseology being 'What height was the man?', but Coroner Macdonald had already made it clear who was in charge of proceedings. Had Inspector Abberline previously discussed with the Coroner his private theory concerning a tall man, and if so, how convenient would it be if the latest sighting were of a person of similar build?

Inspector Abberline, having already interviewed Caroline Maxwell, was fully aware of her inability to give an accurate description of the man, exactly as she had testified, but perhaps a 'tall' prompt may have guided her answer towards a margin for doubt. Definitely not, whereupon Inspector Abberline jumped to his feet and almost doubled the distance of the sighting from sixteen yards to twenty five, to cast doubt on the accuracy of the description. Caroline Maxwell was proving to be a problem.

The next witness to be asked the same leading question was Sarah Lewis, a laundress, who had seen Mary Kelly with a man at around 2.30 am that morning.

Coroner: Was he a tall man?
Lewis: He was short, pale faced, with a black moustache, small. His age was about forty.'

Definitely not the answer Inspector Abberline had wanted to hear, but, once again, having interviewed Sarah Lewis already, he knew the answer to the question. The Coroner obviously didn't, but had felt compelled to ask the same leading question, on the understanding that such was the man Abberline was seeking. Street gossip, discussed at the inquest, had it that someone had heard a cry of 'Murder' very early in the morning, but enquiries soon revealed that such cries were commonplace in this locality, as reported in the press.

The desire to be interesting has had its effect on the people who live in the Dorset Street Court and lodging houses, and for whatever causes to listen, there are a hundred highly circumstantial stories, which, when carefully sifted, prove to be totally devoid of truth. One woman who lived in the Court stated that about two o'clock she heard a cry of 'Murder'. This story soon became popular, until at least half a dozen women were retelling it as their own personal experience. Each story contradicted the others with respect to the time at which the cry

Mary Jane's date with Michael Maybrick had been organised the day before, with the incentive of the same promise made a month earlier to Mary Ann Kelly, that he would reveal the name of the Whitechapel killer, allowing Mary Jane to claim the reward. He had, of course, to remain undercover. After all, a vigilante couldn't be seen associating too closely with a prostitute, 'albeit a very pretty one like you, Mary Jane.' He would probably arrive in disguise.

Caroline Maxwell was an excellent witness, of sound character, confident and totally convincing. She had not only seen Mary Jane between eight and nine in the morning, but had engaged her in conversation, which confused the court, as Caroline's evidence would conflict with medical opinions as to the estimated time of death. According to the statement of Caroline Maxwell,

The Britannia Public House, Corner of Dorset Street.

Mary Jane Kelly was standing close to the corner of Dorset Street and Commercial Street, secretly waiting for her date to arrive, suffering from a bad hangover, and feeling ill at having to get out of bed so early. She downed a beer in the Britannia Public House, and unsurprisingly threw it up at around 8.30 am. Caroline Maxwell had further confirmed that it was unusual to see Mary Jane so early in the morning, bearing in mind that Caroline made the same trip to Bishopsgate every day at the same time, as Michael Maybrick well knew. Mary Jane was there for a specific reason, a bundle of nervous energy, giddy at the prospect of earning a thousand pounds reward for naming Jack the Ripper. It had not been difficult for the smiling assassin to exploit the poor girl's vulnerability, convincing her that he came from a rich family, and didn't need the money. This was the beginning of a new life for Mary Jane Kelly.

Less than a week earlier, on the 3rd November, an article had appeared on the front page of the popular periodical Illustrated Police News, relating to the activities of undercover detectives patrolling the streets of Whitechapel in women's attire, hoping to entrap Jack the Ripper. The article had not passed unnoticed by the intrepid founder of St Jude's Vigilance Association, avidly devouring all press reports on his uncanny ability to escape detection.

A DISGUISED DETECTIVE, READY FOR THE WHITECHAPEL MONSTER

On the morning of the 10th November, in St. Jude's Church, only a couple of hundred yards away along Commercial Street, Michael Maybrick was in truly theatrical mode. This was to be the piece de resistance. Having already established Caroline Maxwell's daily routine and regular half hour absence, he was confident of a safe period in which to enter Dorset Street, then Miller's Court, when very few people, if any, were around that time of morning. He was, of course, correct. In Dorset Street, where the economy was based on night-time activities, very few people went to bed before 2.00 am, and nearly all were late risers. The killer had planned well, and was in total control. On with the wig, coat, and the hat, only this time it would be different. The wig was long and grey, and the hat was a bonnet, with the big ladies' skirt providing sufficient room to bend his knees, and drop to five feet four inches when stooping. The weapons would be well concealed, with walking stick and old bag containing firewood completing the outfit. Were Michael Maybrick to be detected, Mary Jane would doubtless co-operate, and be most amused to confirm his tales of disguise as a vigilante. In the event, not one of the few people around at the time gave a second glance at the old crone, hobbling along Commercial Street at a snail's pace. Mary Jane met him in fits of laughter, slipped him the key, and hovered around the Britannia pub in Commercial Street until Caroline returned, just as she was told. What an adventure! Maybrick entered the room unseen, took off the woman's attire to reveal his own clothes, and began the process of burning the hat, wig and skirt in the fire. Once Mary Jane returned, Michael Maybrick would have put her at ease, suggesting a cup of tea, and tending the fire in the grate, allowing it to really build up in intensity. Inspector Abberline at the inquest revealed the disposal of the evidence, without interpreting the significance of the find.

Insp. Abberline: There were traces of a large fire being kept up in the grate, so much that it had melted the spout of the kettle off. We have since gone through the ashes in the fireplace. There were remains of clothing, a portion of a brim of a hat, and a skirt, and it appeared as if a large quantity of women's clothing had been burned.
Coroner: Can you give a reason why they have been burned?
Insp. Abberline: I can only imagine that it was to make a light for the man to see what he was doing.

According to Caroline Maxwell's reliable witness statement, Mary Jane Kelly was alive at 8.45 am. The scene was set for the completion of the Funny Little Game, and even better, Mary Jane looked remarkably like brother James's harlot of a wife. Yes, this would be Florie, who he would now hack and dismember to his heart's content.

The key and the burnt clothes puzzle them.   Ha, ha.
I had a key, and with it I did flee.
The hat I did burn, for light I did yearn,
And I thought of the whoring mother.   Diary of Jack the Ripper.

Soon the fire would be blazing, kettle on top.   'Why not take off
your clothes, Mary Jane, whilst I pour the tea?'   Mary Jane's
clothes were laid out neatly, including the same red pelerine cape
she was wearing earlier that morning, a further indication that the
burnt remnants in the fireplace belonged to the killer.   Like most
poor Whitechapel prostitutes, the only garments owned by Mary
Jane Kelly would have been those she wore every day.

The clothes of the woman were lying by the side of the bed, as
though they had been taken off and laid down in the ordinary
manner.   The Times. 10 November 1888.

This was the culmination of Michael Maybrick's ultimate fantasy,
his final victim manipulated into a situation of total domination
and control.   His first totally naked woman, his to do with as he
wished. The Museum of Anatomy.   Jack the Ripper leaned over
Mary Jane's naked body with a reassuring smile, slashing her
throat from ear to ear, leaning back to relish the blood spurting
onto the bed and the wall behind.

Dr. Phillips, on his arrival, carefully examined the body of the
dead woman, and later made a second examination in company
with Dr. Bond from Westminster, Dr. Gordon Brown from the
City, and Dr. Phillips' assistant.   The Star. 10 November 1888.

Lodged in Home Office files is the following statement by Dr.
Thomas Bond.

Rigor mortis had set in, but increased during the process of examination. From this it is difficult to say, with any degree of certainty, the exact time that had elapsed since death, as the period varies from six to twelve hours before rigidity sets in. The body was comparatively cold at two o'clock, and the remains of a meal were found in the stomach, and scattered about over the intestines. It is, therefore, pretty certain that the woman must have been dead for about twelve hours, and the partly digested food would indicate that death took place about three or four hours after the food was taken, so one or two o'clock in the morning would be the probable time of murder.

HO144/221/A49301C.

This time of death is in direct contradiction to the testimony of Caroline Maxwell, who was adamant that not only had she seen Mary Jane Kelly between 8 am and 9 am, but had engaged her in conversation. Dr. Bond's evidence is based on opinion with an admitted degree of uncertainty, changing from 'six to twelve hours', to 'pretty certainly twelve hours', to concur with the incorrectly supposed time of murder at 3.00 am. Such vaguery is accounted for by Dr. Bond's own admission, 'It is difficult to say, with any degree of certainty, the exact time that had elapsed since death.' In other words, neither doctor knew for certain. As for the rate of food digestion, Mary Jane could have eaten at any time during the night, and it has no real relevance, particularly as Mary Jane was seen vomiting in the morning.

Dr. Bond seemed to have disregarded, or been unaware of the fact, that a blazing fire had been raging in the grate that morning. Warm conditions speed up the onset of rigor mortis, and the intense fire would have provided a favourable environment for the stimulation of the physiological processes. Furthermore, the accepted medical formulae for loss of bodily heat would simply not have applied to what was effectively an empty carcass.

Owing to the loss of blood, the body would have got cold quickly,
but a big fire appears to have been kept up, as the police say that
when they entered the room it was quite warm.

The Star. 12 November 1888.

The fire had died out well before Dr. Bond's arrival, and the door
had been open for half an hour on an icy November day, with the
inside temperature soon equating with the cold air outside.   Dr.
Bond had evidently not factored the earlier sustained heat into his
calculations, noting the body was 'comparatively cold,' unaware
of the fact that it had only been cold for half an hour, prior to
which it had been heated to ambient room temperature for some
considerable time, accelerating the onset and rate of rigor mortis.
A modern authority on the subject, Dr. K.S. Saladin, states,

Rigor mortis is one of the recognisable signs of death, caused by
chemical changes in the muscles post mortem, which cause the
limbs of the corpse to stiffen.   In humans, rigor mortis can occur
as soon as four hours post mortem.

Anatomy & Physiology. 6th Edition. 2010. McGraw Hill.

Given Dr. Bond's later inspection of the body, some time after
Dr. Phillips' initial inspection, say around 2.00 pm or 2.30 pm,
this modern interpretation would allow for a time of death
between 10.00 am and 10.30 am, around an hour and a half after
Caroline Maxwell's last encounter with Mary Jane at 8.45 am,
ample time for Maybrick to desecrate the corpse, given that the
body was not discovered until 10.45 am.

Dr. Bagster Phillips testified that 'severance of the right carotid
artery was inflicted while the deceased was lying on the right side
of the bed.'   Previous throat slitting had been from the rear of the
victim, cutting left to right with the right hand.   This time, the cut
commenced at the right carotid artery.   The deranged psychopath

had stared directly into the blue eyes of his victim as he slashed her throat. Terrible damage was inflicted, with most of the face cut away, but the eyes of Florence Maybrick were left untouched, gazing at him as he set about his maniacal dissection to new depths of depravity, totally desecrating Mary Jane's naked body. Murder was insufficient, this was an act of punishment, personal vengeance on the whore. To quote the words of Bro. Sir Charles Warren, 'The key to the whole subject may be found in the Book of Ezekiel.' Michael Maybrick had indulged his wildest fantasies in accordance with divine instructions from his mentor. The fire had been so intense that, according to Inspector Abberline's testimony, it had melted the spout off the brass kettle, the contents of which were never revealed.

Blow the fire upon it, to melt it, so will I gather you in mine anger and my fury, and I will leave you there and melt you. Set on a pot, set it on, and also pour water into it, gather the pieces thereof into it, even every good piece, the thigh and the shoulder ... make it boil well... Bring it out piece by piece. For her blood is in the midst of her, I will even make the pile for the fire great. Heap on wood, kindle the fire, consume the flesh ... Then set it empty upon the coals thereof, that the brass of it may be hot, and may burn, and that the filthiness of it may be molten in it.

Ezekiel. Chapter 23.

Immediately following Inspector Abberline's evidence, there followed a quite remarkable occurrence, as Coroner Roderick McDonald addressed the jury,

The question is whether you will adjourn for further evidence. My own opinion is that it is very unnecessary for two courts to deal with these cases, and go through the evidence time after time, which only causes expense and time. If the Coroner's jury can come to a decision as to the cause of death, then that is all they have to do. It is for you to say whether you will close the inquiry today; if not, we shall adjourn for a week or a fortnight, to hear the evidence you desire.

The jury foreman, without any consultation with his fellow jurors, stood up and announced that sufficient evidence had been provided to give a verdict of 'Wilful murder against some person or persons unknown'. Coroner McDonald then, without further ado, arbitrarily terminated the inquest, attracting controversy and criticism from all quarters. Dr. Thomas Bond had not been called upon to testify, and neither had medical evidence been provided by Dr. Bagster Phillips as to the nature of the injuries, or the likely means by which they were inflicted. As a consequence, there is no official record of the injuries inflicted on Mary Jane Kelly, only newspaper reports. The Daily Telegraph was the first off the mark to criticise not only this withholding of information, but the subterfuge employed to thwart further action.

A second inquest would have been held on the body had it been removed into the Whitechapel district for burial. Mr. Wynn Baxter states that in that case it could not have been avoided, but the double action has been averted by the action of Mr. H. Wilton, parish clerk and keeper of the Shoreditch mortuary. He has obtained from the Coroner's officer an order to prepare the coffin. Much surprise is expressed that the inquest should have been closed before an opportunity was given to the relatives of the deceased to identify the body. Dr. Macdonald stated that the duty of the jury was to ascertain the cause of death, but the common law, since Edward I, has declared that 'all the injuries of the body, also all wounds, ought to be viewed, and the length, breadth and degrees, with what weapon, and in what part of the body the wound is, and how many wounds there be, and who gave the wounds', all things that must be enrolled in the roll of the Coroner. No question was put as to any of these points. It is in the power of the Attorney-General to apply to the High Court of Justice to hold a new inquest, if he is satisfied that there has been

197

rejection of evidence, irregularity of proceedings, or insufficient of inquiry. This course is improbable, as it is stated that Mr. Phillips, the divisional surgeon of police, with whom the Coroner consulted in private, has held a commission from the Home Office for some time, and he does not consider himself a 'free agent'.

Daily Telegraph. 14 November 1888.

Overnight discussions had been taking place behind closed doors between Whitehall officials and Dr. Bagster Phillips, on the wounds inflicted on Mary Jane's body. The clumsy manner in which the facts were suppressed is an indication of the panic within the Establishment, and all indications are that the official Coroner, Dr. Wynne Baxter, had been replaced by a more compliant officer, who, in collusion with the jury foreman, had arbitrarily determined the inquest to be terminated, with no further consultation.

Some surprise was created among those present at the inquest in Shoreditch Town Hall by the abrupt termination of the inquiry, as it was well known that further evidence would be forthcoming. The Coroner himself distinctly told the jury that he was only going to take the preliminary portion of Dr. G. B. Phillips's evidence, the remainder of which would be more fully given at the adjourned inquiry. No question was put to Dr. Phillips as the mutilated remains of the body, and the Coroner did not think fit to ask the doctor whether any portions of the body were missing. The doctor stated to the jury during the inquiry that his examination was not yet completed. Notwithstanding reports to the contrary, it is still confidently asserted that some of the portions of the body of the deceased woman are missing.

The Times. 13 November 1888.

Had Dr. Bagster Phillips discovered portions of boiled flesh amongst the body parts? Did this explain the dire necessity to terminate the public dissemination of just what did lie behind the door of 13 Miller's Court?

M. BAYNARD

The feeling of euphoria on the morning of Lord Mayor's Day was surpassed only by the satisfaction of having completed the Funny Little Game without detection. Michael Maybrick considered himself invincible, semi-divine perhaps, a true disciple of Ezekiel. He had made greater headlines than the Lord Mayor's Parade and the King's birthday, and Sir Charles Warren had finally surrendered.

Dorset Street was the first occasion on which Michael Maybrick had killed in daylight, face to face with his victim. The blue eyes were imprinted on his brain, and wouldn't go away. Much as he fought against it, he was being drawn into an obsession with the blue eyes of Florence Maybrick, although incapable of consummating his desire. Family friend Florence Aunspaugh is quoted as saying of Florence,

The crowning glory of her person was her hair. It was blonde, but not the faded out type of yellow, it had just enough of a tinge of red in it to make it a glossy rich golden. Mrs. Maybrick's eyes were the most beautiful blue I have ever seen. They were such a very deep blue that at times they were violet, but the expression was most peculiar, you would focus your eyes on hers with a steady gaze. They would appear to be entirely without life or expression, as if you were gazing into the eyes of a corpse, totally void of animation or expression ... At no time was there any expression of intellectuality, either in eyes or face, yet there was a magnetic charm about her countenance that greatly attracted one and seemed irresistible. Florence Aunspaugh. Letters to Trevor Christie.

Edwin had already confided in Michael about his flirtations with Florence, little realising the fire he was stoking inside the unstable head of his brother, Jack the Ripper. Edwin didn't have a clue, but perhaps Florence had an inkling that her iceberg of a brother-in-law was perfectly capable of murder.   Conversation around the Whitechapel murders would have been inevitable in the Liverpool household, particularly as James had been in London, at Michael's invitation, over the last fateful weekend, and possibly earlier ones.   Florence must have pondered over the coincidences, and the seeds of doubt may well have been sown. Perhaps Florence, not renowned for her discretion, had ventured to James the suggestion that she would not have been the slightest bit surprised if Michael was the Whitechapel Murderer.   Perhaps James himself had also begun to harbour doubts, after all no-one knew Michael better than James, with a lifetime's experience of his older brother's weird behavioural patterns.   Michael had never approved of the marriage, and made no secret to James of the fact that he considered it a big mistake.   In fact he had already decided that Florence would be the next subject of his attention, after all she not only possessed the necessary 'MA' in her name, but the full 'MAYBRICK'.

James too could perhaps prove a problem, and his fate was also in the balance.   Psychopaths are completely devoid of sentiment, family ties mean nothing and a sinister plan was evolving.

On Monday, 12th November, three days after the murder of Mary Jane Kelly, a letter with London postmark was received at King's Cross Police Station. On the lower left of the letter, in inverted commas, were two

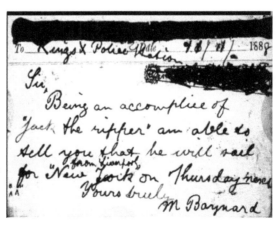

small but foreboding inverted 'V's, disconcertingly similar to those intentionally sliced into the cheeks of Mary Ann Kelly.

Sir,

Being an accomplice of 'Jack the Ripper', am able to tell you that he will sail for New York from Liverpool on Thursday next.

Yours truly
M. Baynard.

Herewith another obtuse reference to the Cunard sailings from Liverpool, similar to those contained within the earlier Diego Laurenz postcard. The latest Cunard advert held more scope for mischief. Sailings from Liverpool to New York took place on Tuesdays and Saturdays, and 'Thursday next' was the 22nd November, on which day the S.S. Pavonia sailed from Liverpool, not for New York but for Boston, under Captain Alexander McKay, whose five letter surname is contained within the eight letters of 'Maybrick'. Both the earlier Diego Laurenz postcard and the Baynard letter contained clues, but engaged deliberate misdirection.

Not 'to New York', but 'from New York' in the previous Diego Laurenz postcard.   Captain McMickan. Five 'Maybrick' letters. Not 'for New York', but 'for Boston' in the present Baynard letter. Captain McKay. Five 'Maybrick' letters.

Maybrick had also included five letters of his surname within the signature M. Baynard, MAYBR, a fitting sequel to the BRICK hidden within the previous letter of the 23rd October.   So obtuse were these deliberately contrived 'clues' that only Michael Maybrick understood them, gloating in the knowledge that they, like his murderous alter ego, were hidden in plain sight, a reassurance of his supreme self-belief and everyone else's stupidity. A closer look at the disguised handwriting reveals two points worthy of examination.   Referring once again to the National Census records of 1911, completed by Michael Maybrick in his own hand, there is a marked similarity between the distinctive letters 'S' in 'Sir' and 'Slingo', and 'Ne' in 'New York' and 'Nellie'.

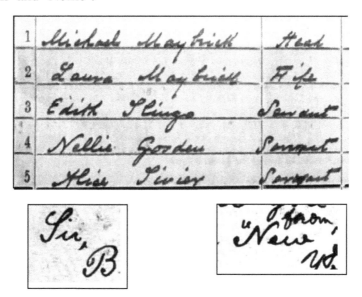

Next, the flowery and articulate letter 'B', seen in the Dear Boss letter and twice in the Baynard letter, is worthy of special attention. Bearing in mind the ongoing attempts at disguised handwriting, it is all but identical to the letter 'B' in the letter handed in to the police after the Liz Chapman murder, threatening Israel Schwartz, (see below), and signed 'Jack the Ripper', linking the Baynard letter to the killer of Liz Stride.

Mr. Baynard is a character in 'The Expeditions of Humphrey Clinker', a novel by Tobias Smollett, published in 1771. Baynard's wife, in Michael Maybrick's eyes, equated in many ways with Florence Maybrick, who had stolen the heart of his brother James, and was slowly doing the same to his bank balance. The eerie parallel with Baynard's marriage reflects his own views on Florence.

'She could read, and write, and dance, and sing, and play upon the harpsichord, and smatter French, and fake a hand at whist and ombre, but even these accomplishments she possessed in halves. She excels in nothing. Her conversation was flat, her style mean, and her expression embarrassed. In a word, her character was totally insipid. Her person was not disagreeable, but there was nothing graceful in her address, nor engaging in her manners. Baynard had flattered himself that it be no difficult matter to mould such a subject after his own fashion, and that she

would cheerfully enter into his views, which were wholly turned to domestic happiness. This, however, was a visionary scheme, which he never was able to realise. His wife was as ignorant as a new-born babe of everything that related to the conduct of the family. Her understanding did not reach so far as to comprehend the first principles of discretion, but her ruling passion was vanity, not that species which arises from self-conceit of superior accomplishments, but that which is of a bastard and idiot nature, excited by show and ostentation, with not even the least consciousness of any merit.'

The Expeditions of Humphrey Clinker. Tobias Smollett.

This was a smug swipe at Florence which only Michael Maybrick understood. No-one else needed to know, but the postcard served as a release valve for the turmoil in his hyper-active mindset. The hatred was simmering. The clock was ticking. Florence was in deep trouble.

GRAND ORGANIST

Few Freemasons of the time would have progressed beyond the three introductory degrees of the United Grand Lodge of England, followed by exaltation into the Chapter of the Supreme Grand Charter of Royal Arch Freemasons.   There are, however, other side Orders, including the Knights Templar and the Rose Croix, or Ancient and Accepted Rite, under whose auspices further degrees are confirmed, culminating in the exclusive 33rd degree. Two powerful figureheads were prominent within the higher echelons, namely   the   Earl of   Latham and Colonel Henry Shadwell Clerke.

THE EARL OF LATHOM.

Bro. The Earl of Latham, Deputy Grand Master of the United Grand Lodge of England, held the equivalent rank within the Supreme Grand Chapter of Royal Arch Freemasons, and was Sovereign Grand Commander of the Supreme Grand Council of the Ancient and Accepted Rite, 33rd degree. He was also the Lord Chamberlain of England, liaison officer in the corridors of power between the House of Lords and Her Majesty Queen Victoria, responsible for state visits, investitures, and the State Opening of Parliament.

COLONEL HENRY SHADWELL CLERKE.

Bro. Henry Shadwell Clerke, Grand Secretary of the United Grand Lodge of England, held the equivalent rank within the Supreme Royal Arch, and was Grand Secretary and Grand Chancellor of the Supreme Council of the Ancient and Accepted Rite, 33rd degree.

Our Grand Secretary's conception of duty was that it included not only the recording of minutes, attending meetings, receiving money, but likewise the post of adviser-in-chief to the Grand Master, who from his more intimate acquaintance with the inner life of the Lodges and Chapters, was more competent than any official of Grand Lodge to be the guide, philosopher and friend of that most illustrious personage. The Freemason. 2 January 1892.

Effectively, Bro. the Earl of Lathom was confidant and adviser to Her Majesty Queen Victoria, whilst Bro. Col. Shadwell Clerke had the ear of his Royal Highness, the Prince of Wales. These extremely influential Brethren, responsible for maintaining the status quo within Freemasonry, were senior members of the prestigious St. George Chapter No.42 of the Ancient and Accepted Rite, which, during the Earl's lifetime, was the most authoritative convocation within Freemasonry, the Masonic equivalent of the Privy Council, comprising twenty eight members, including two QC's and six Brethren of the 33rd degree, of whom four were members of the nine strong Supreme Council.

The United Grand Lodge and Supreme Royal Arch were based at Great Queen Street in Covent Garden, whilst the Supreme Council of the Ancient and Accepted Rite, 33rd Degree, met at 33 Golden Square, St James's, referred to by members simply as 'St James's'.

Another member of St. George's Chapter No.42, testament to the man's unshakable self-belief and convincing ability to feign sincerity, was Bro. Michael Maybrick, who had been awarded the rank of 30th degree following his year in office in 1887. So how did the parish clerk's son from Liverpool, turned serial killer, manage to infiltrate this most elite of Masonic convocations?

Ten years earlier, at the consecration of Orpheus Lodge, one of Michael Maybrick's co-founders was Bro. Frederic Davison, a prominent member of the illustrious St George's Chapter 42. The Grand Lodge Representative at the inauguration ceremony was Captain Nathaniel G. Phillips, Sovereign Grand Commander of the Ancient and Accepted Rite, Gentleman Usher to Her Majesty Queen Victoria, and senior member St. George's Chapter 42. Bonds had been formed, friendships cultivated, and the introduction was assured.

The Earl of Lathom, in addition to his London appointment, was Provincial Grand Master of Lancashire, and a member of the highly respected St. George's Lodge of Harmony No.32, Liverpool, of which James Maybrick had occupied the position of Lodge Secretary for some years, during which time he would have encountered the Earl on a number of occasions, a fact which had not passed unnoticed by Michael Maybrick.

In November 1888, Bro. Michael Maybrick was notified of his impending promotion in the New Year to the office of Grand Organist of the United Grand Lodge of England, and similar rank within the Supreme Grand Chapter of Royal Arch Masons. Also in line for promotion was Bro. Col. Robert Edis, confidant of HRH the Prince of Wales, and Commanding Officer of the 20th Middlesex (Artists) Rifle Volunteers, another source of Bro. Maybrick's meteoric rise into the elite circles of Freemasonry.

The big event was not due to happen until the following April, but overnight Michael Maybrick became a dedicated Freemason. The Funny Little Game was over, and the associated Masonic jibes were a thing of the past, now he had deposed the pompous Bro. Sir Charles Warren. On reflection, Brother Maybrick would shortly occupy a higher Masonic rank than the retired Commissioner, so in many ways the tables would soon be reversed. Jack the Ripper was confined to the past. Herein lay a new direction to the social standing craved by the boy from Church Alley, the most notorious man in the land, concealed under the cloak of irreproachable respectability.

It is widely believed that a high proportion of serving officers within the Metropolitan Police were Freemasons at the time of the Whitechapel murders, but such was not the case. Author Keith Skinner, in 'The Jack the Ripper Source Book' has listed the senior police officials at the time, in alphabetical order.

Frederick Abberline	Inspector, C.I.D.
Dr. Robert Anderson	Asst. Commissioner, C.I.D.
Walter Andrews	Inspector, Metropolitan Police
Thomas Arnold	Head, Whitechapel, H Division
Walter Beck	Inspector, Metropolitan Police
Alexander Bruce	Senior Asst. Commissioner, Met. Pol.

Joseph Chandler	Deputy Inspector, H. Division
Edward Collard	Inspector, Metropolitan Police
Charles Cutbush	Executive Supt., Scotland Yard
Ernest Ellisdon	Inspector, Metropolitan Police
Alfred Foster	Supt., City of London Police
Sir James Fraser	Commissioner, City of London Police
Joseph Helson	Inspector, Metropolitan Police
John Littlechild	Chief Inspector, Metropolitan Police
James McWilliam	Inspector
James Munro	Commissioner Metropolitan Police
Col. Bolton Monsell	Constable, Metropolitan Police
Henry Moore	Inspector, C.I.D.
Edmund Reid	H Division, Metropolitan Police
John Shore	Superintendent, Metropolitan Police
Major Henry Smith	Acting Commissioner, City of London
John Spratling	Inspector, Metropolitan Police
Donald Swanson	Chief Inspector, C.I.D.
Sir Charles Warren	Chief Commissioner, Met. Police
John West	Inspector
Adolphus Williamson	Chief Constable

Of these officers, only five were Freemasons at the time of the Ripper murders, namely Warren, Williamson, Swanson, Helson and Reid. Hence the reason why Bro. Sir Charles Warren had insisted that all material relevant to the Whitechapel murders be dealt with by Bro. Donald Swanson, assisted by Bro. Adolphus Williamson, who would deal with all references to the possible connection between the Ripper and the Freemasons behind closed doors in Bro. Swanson's office. This, of course, left Inspector Abberline on the outside, which may have accounted for his reticence in sharing any more information than was absolutely necessary. Ironically, the real influence behind any protective measures to limit collateral damage resulting from a possible Masonic connection lay in the hands of Bro. The Earl of Lathom, the Lord Chamberlain, the very person who had just promoted Bro. Michael Maybrick into the ranks of the Masonic elite.

The Home Secretary, Henry Matthews, and his Permanent Under-Secretary Sir Godfrey Lushingham, were not Freemasons, but were in regular contact with the Lord Chamberlain, acting as liaison officers between Crown and Government. The Whitechapel Murderer was a constant topic of conversation, and who is to say what was discussed behind closed doors? There were certainly ways and means of influencing events, as instanced by the inexplicable termination of the Mary Jane Kelly inquest, most definitely ordered by a higher authority, and attracting widespread criticism from all quarters, especially in legal circles. Word even began to spread that the identity of the murderer was known.

We have heard the wildest stories as to the reason which popular opinion in Whitechapel assigns for Mr. Matthews' obstinate refusal to offer a reward. It is believed by people who pass among their neighbours as sensible folk that the Government do not want the murderer to be convicted, that they are interested in concealing his identity, that in fact they know it, and will not divulge it. The Star. 10 November 1888.

On the 31st December 1888, a badly decomposed body was recovered from the River Thames at Chiswick. The body was identified as that of thirty one year old Montague John Druitt, whose jacket contained stones and a rail ticket, stamped 1st December 1888, providing a good indication of the date of death. Testifying at the inquest, his brother William stated that Montague had been dismissed from his post at Blackheath School for undisclosed reasons, and that a letter addressed to him, found at the victim's residence, stated, 'Since Friday, I felt I was going to be like mother, and the best thing for me to do was die.' William Druitt then advised that his mother had been declared insane the previous July. Interestingly, the Scotland Yard file on the case reads,

Mr. M.J. Druitt, said to be a doctor of good character, who disappeared at the time of the Miller's Court murder and whose body, which was said to have been upwards of a month in the water, was found in the Thames on 31st December, or about seven weeks after the murder. He was sexually insane, and from private information I have little doubt that his own family believed him to be the murderer.

No more murders had taken place in Whitechapel since the 9th November, and it suited some to name Druitt as the Whitechapel Murderer, entirely without foundation, but it certainly helped to stem rumours of a cover-up.

Commissioner Robert Anderson and Inspector Donald Swanson held their own opinions that Aaron Kosminski was the murderer, and Druitt and Kosminski are cited as possible culprits to this day. Intriguingly, but unsurprisingly, whilst the names George Lusk and Joseph Aarons, members of the Whitechapel Vigilance Committee, were quoted in the press on a number of occasions, no records exist of any named member of the St. Jude's Vigilance Association in church annals, the Toynbee Record, or in press reports of the time.

In just a few months time, Bro. Michael Maybrick would be Grand Organist at the keyboard of the mighty organ in the magnificent Grand Temple in Great Queen Street, London, before one thousand seven hundred Freemasons, a position previously occupied by his musical colleague Bro. Sir Arthur Sullivan. Given the influential contacts within St. George's

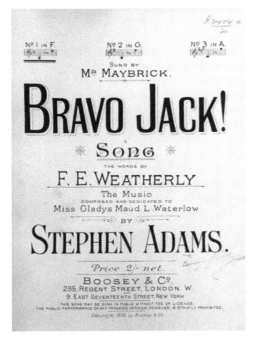

Chapter No.42, distant dreams of a knighthood were nearing reality. The organs of St. Peter's and St. Jude's had been steps on the stairway to fame, and a bright future beckoned, a future that could not be compromised.

Before long all England will know the name I have given myself. It is indeed a name to remember. I shall be, before long, on every person's lips within the land. Perhaps her gracious Majesty will become acquainted with it. I wonder if she will honour me with a knighthood. The Diary of Jack the Ripper.

Yours truly
Jack the Ripper
Dont mind me giving the trade name

THE SEQUEL

Following the last murder in November, Whitechapel slowly returned to squalid normality. Michael Maybrick kept a low profile, but still harboured a psychotic fixation with sister-in-law Florence, and a nagging concern that brother James knew, or suspected, too much about his nefarious activities. There follows a saga of intrigue, mystery and deception, culminating in one of the most gripping and controversial trials in British criminal law.

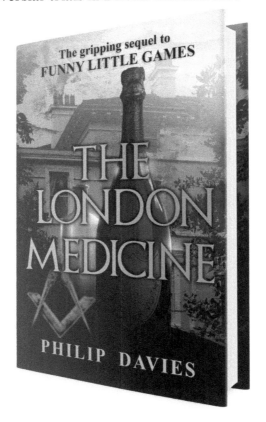

**READ ON FOR AN EXTRACT
FROM THIS GRIPPING SEQUEL**

Within less than a quarter of a mile of Dorset Street, where on the morning of last Lord Mayor's Day the mutilated body of Mary Jane Kelly was discovered, another brutal murder was committed on Wednesday morning, bringing up the horrible toll of Whitechapel outrages to eight. Running from Wentworth Street into Whitechapel Road is a by-alley known as Old Castle Street, which is used by costermongers of the neighbourhood for storing wheelbarrows and other miscellaneous vehicles at the close of each working day. Here, as in Mitre Square, the police patrol is timed to pass every few minutes, a circumstance which lends corroboration to the theory that this was the work of the hand which has already laid low several women of the same locality. Shortly before 1 o'clock, a constable, while passing through Castle Alley, Whitechapel, noticed a woman lying in the shadow of a doorway. He was horrified to discover she was dead, blood flowing from a wound in the throat. The wound was so deep and clean that there can be little doubt that it was inflicted by a razor or equally sharp instrument. The woman, who appeared to be about 40 years of age, lay upon her back, her clothes were turned above the waist and on the stomach an incised wound of considerable dimensions had been inflicted.

East London Advertiser. 20 July 1889.

The victim of the murder was about forty-five years of age, and was about five foot four inches in height. She had brown hair and eyes, and a fair complexion. She is believed to have been of the 'unfortunate' class, but has not yet been identified. Several hours elapsed before the woman was identified, but a man named John McCormack came forward during the day, and recognised her as Alice Mackenzie, with whom he had lived for six or seven years, and who has for some time lodged with him as his wife.

The Western Times. 18 July 1889.

A clay pipe was found next to the body, which McCormack explained as belonging to the deceased, who smoked a great deal, accounting for her street name 'Clay Pipe Alice.' Intimate knowledge of the locality was indicated by the murder scene being located on the boundary line between two police districts. Officers from Leman Street Police station,

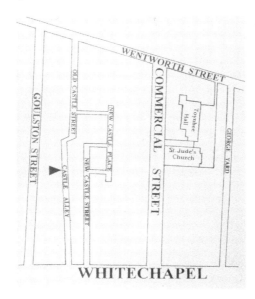

WHITECHAPEL

patrolling Whitechapel High Street in the course of their beat, did not enter Castle Alley, which at that end was scarcely wider than a doorway, allowing a covert vantage position from whence to assess a safe escape. Officers from Bishopsgate Police Station, on the other hand, would routinely enter from Wentworth Street at the north end of the alley, announcing their presence by the echo of hob-nailed boots, allowing ample warning for the assassin to effect a casual exit into Whitechapel High Street, while the policeman was still wending his way towards the body. Furthermore, the passageway, 180 yards in length, was dog-legged, and whilst an approaching policeman could be heard, there was no direct line of sight from Wentworth Street into the lower end of Castle Alley. A meticulously planned choice of location.

The previous evening, Alice Mackenzie had been drinking in a public house close to the Cambridge Music Hall in Commercial Street, a haunt of the balladeer Michael Maybrick, just up the road from Toynbee Hall and St. Jude's

Church. There Alice was singled out, already having been shortlisted as part of the previous year's Funny Little Game, encountered in the course of patrols as a trusted member of St. Jude's Vigilance Association. With the obligatory letters 'MA' and the letter 'K' in her name, Alice may well have been on the list as the final victim of the Funny Little Game, until Mary Jane Kelly appeared on cue, bearing such an uncanny resemblance to Florence. In the assassin's eyes, Alice had simply benefited from a stay of execution. Once back in Whitechapel for the first time in months, the urge for retribution had been triggered.The uncontrollable craving for bloody retribution, the thrill of the escape, and the glory of the newspaper headlines. Euphoria.

Three days later, crowds gathered, following an unrelated minor assault case close to the murder scene,

Screams of 'Jack the Ripper' and 'Murder', soon attracted attention, and crowds of men and women ran from all directions to the spot whence the screams proceeded. Amongst those who first arrived on the scene were several men of the local Vigilance Association, who have only just recommenced their work.

The Times. 20 July 1889.

In a letter to Assistant Commissioner Robert Anderson, after having examined the body, Dr. Bond wrote,

I see in this murder evidence of similar design to the former Whitechapel murders, viz sudden onslaught on the prostrate woman, the throat skilfully and resolutely cut with subsequent mutilation, each mutilation indicating sexual thoughts and a desire to mutilate the abdomen and sexual organs. I am of the opinion that the murder was performed by the same person who committed the former series of Whitechapel Murders.

Dr. Thomas Bond.

As a further endorsement of Dr. Bond's opinion, Sir Charles Warren's successor, Commissioner James Monro, having examined the corpse soon after its discovery, wrote in his initial report,

I need not say that every effort will be made by the police to discover the murderer, who, I am inclined to believe, is identical with the notorious 'Jack the Ripper', of last year.

Commissioner James Munro.

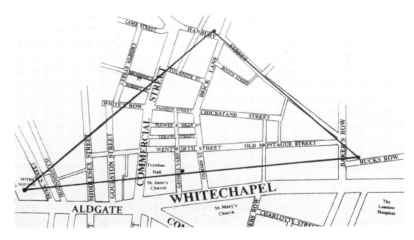

Alice Mackenzie, unsurprisingly, had not been picked at random, possessing as she did the necessary MA requirement, but this choice of victim was the assassin's piece de resistance. Not only were the first nine consecutive letters of ALICE MACKENZIE included in MICHAEL MAYBRICK, but ALICE contained five of the seven letters in MICHAEL, and MACKENZIE contained five of the eight in MAYBRICK. Furthermore, as an irrefutable proof of Michael Maybrick's meticulous forward planning, the Castle Alley murder site was planned exactly on the line between Mitre Square, George Yard and Buck's Row.

Totally unaware of this clever little game, Bro. The Earl of Lathom was beginning to realise there were serious flaws in the convincingly sincere story confided in him months earlier by the Grand Organist, Bro. Michael Maybrick. James Maybrick may well be dead, but Jack the Ripper was not, and Freemasonry was still under threat from the revelation that the Whitechapel Murderer was a member of the Order.

Acknowledgements

As a Freemason of over forty years standing, and a longstanding member of James Maybrick's Liverpool Masonic Chapter, my interest in possible connections to the Whitechapel Murders has been ongoing for a similar length of time, inspired by the publication of Shirley Harrison's 'Diary of Jack the Ripper', thereafter pursuing idiosyncrasies and anomalies hitherto unexplored, and deciphering clues left by Michael Maybrick for his own self-gratification. Further inspiration along the way has been provided by Paul Feldman's 'Jack the Ripper, The Final Chapter', and Bruce Robinson's magnificent 'They All Love Jack', both involving in-depth investigation by researcher Keith Skinner. Thanks are due to Robert Smith for words of encouragement over the last couple of years, and gratitude is also extended to the following.

Paul Johnson of the National Archives, Kew. Patrick Baty of the Artists Rifles Association. Peter Aitkenhead of the Library and Museum of Freemasonry. The staff at the British Library, & Liverpool Central Library.

Images are published by courtesy of the following:-

∞ The National Library of Scotland.
∞ Alamy.
∞ The Science Museum.
∞ Robert Smith.
∞ The Carl Rosa Trust.
∞ Look and Learn.
∞ The Museum of Freemasonry.
∞ Tower Hamlets Archives.

∞ The Artists Rifles Association.

∞ Tate Images.

∞ Art UK.

∞ G.F. Watts Gallery.

∞ The British Library Board.

∞ Top Foto.

∞ Barts Health Archives and Museums (Ref RLHINV).

∞ The Government Art Collection.

∞ The Jewish Museum London.

∞ Particularly informative has been the online reference website, Casebook : Jack the Ripper. An excellent source of reference. (www.casebook.org)

∞ The following images are produced by courtesy of the National Archives, Kew. (MEP03-140) (MEP03-142 pt.1) (MEP03/142/2) (MEP03-142 pt.1-139) (MEP03/3159/1) (MEP03-142 pt.3 - 500/521) (HO144-1640-A50678/272)

Most importantly, this book would never have happened without the resilience, perseverance and dedication of my dear wife Elaine, who literally put it all together on the home computer and printer, aided in the final stages by my son Ben. This book is dedicated to you both. Thank you so much.

Special thanks to Kate Coe at Book Polishers, for final additions and amendments.

Book cover design by Philip Davies. Artwork and Graphics by Ken Dawson at Creative Covers (info@ccovers.co.uk).

Bibliography

Dr. David Abrahamson. *The Life of Jack the Ripper*. Robson Books. 1992. Paul Begg. *Jack the Ripper, The Facts*. Robson Books. 2004.

Paul Begg, Martin Fido and Keith Skinner. *The Jack the Ripper A-Z*. Headline Book Publishing. 1994.

David Bernard. *Light on Masonry*. William Williams. Utica, N.Y. 1829.

Gordon Burn. *Somebody's Husband, Somebody's Son*. Faber & Faber. 2004 David Canter, *Mapping Murder*, Virgin Publishing. 2003

Alexander Chisholm, Christopher DiGrazia & Dave Yost. *The News from Whitechapel*. McFarland & Co. 2002

Roger Cross. *The Yorkshire Ripper*. Grafton. 1981

John Douglas and Martin Olshaker. *Mindhunter*. Arrow Books. 2017.

Stuart P. Evans and Keith Skinner. *Jack the Ripper. Letters from Hell*. Sutton Publishing Ltd. 2001.

Stuart P. Evans and Keith Skinner. *The Ultimate Jack the Ripper Source Book*. Constable & Robinson. Ltd. 2000.

Paul Feldman. *The True History of the Diary of Jack the Ripper*. Virgin Publishing Ltd. 1998.

Brian Griffiths and Michael Hedley Hill. *32CCL*. 2005.

Shirley Harrison. *The Diary of Jack the Ripper*. Smith Gryphon Ltd. 1992

Martin Howells and Keith Skinner. *The Ripper Legacy*. Sidgwick & Jackson. 1987.

Seth Linder, Caroline Morris and Keith Skinner. *Ripper Diary*. The History Press Ltd 2003.

Bruce Robinson. *They All Love Jack*. Harper Collins. 2015.

David Rumbelow. *The Complete Jack the Ripper*. W.H. Allen Ltd. 1975

Dr. K.S. Saladin. *Anatomy and Physiology*. 6th Edition. McGraw Hill. 2017.

Robert Smith. *The True History of the Diary of Jack the Ripper*. Mango Books. 2019.

Tom Wescott. *The Bank Holiday Murders*. Tom Wescott. 2014.

Tom Wescott. *Ripper Confidential*. Tom Wescott. 2017.

Richard Whittingtons Egan. *Jack the Ripper. The Definitive Casebook*. Amberley Publishing. 2018

Chronology

25 October 1838	Birth of James Maybrick
3 January 1841	Birth of Michael Maybrick
4 May 1851	Birth of Edwin Maybrick
3 September 1862	Birth of Florence Maybrick
27 July 1881	Marriage of James and Florence Maybrick
1886	Michael Maybrick joins 20th Middlesex Rifles
4 April 1888	Murder of Emma Smith
7 August 1888	Murder of Martha Tabram
31 August 1888	Murder of Mary Ann Nichols
8 September 1888	Murder of Annie Chapman
30 September 1888	Murder of Liz Stride
30 September 1888	Murder of Catherine Eddowes (Mary Ann Kelly)
9 November 1888	Murder of Mary Jane Kelly

Index

N.B.

This list excludes members of the Maybrick family, as this would involve too many references.

Milton Keynes UK
Ingram Content Group UK Ltd.
UKHW020106041123
431801UK00010B/81